The Best
Men's Stage Monologues
of 1995

Other books by Jocelyn A. Beard

100 Men's Stage Monologues from the 1980's
100 Women's Stage Monologues from the 1980's
The Best Men's/Women's Stage Monologues of 1990
The Best Men's/Women's Stage Monologues of 1991
The Best Men's/Women's Stage Monologues of 1992
The Best Men's/Women's Stage Monologues of 1993
The Best Men's/Women's Stage Monologues of 1994
The Best Stage Scenes for Men from the 1980's
The Best Stage Scenes for Women from the 1980's
The Best Stage Scenes of 1992
The Best Stage Scenes of 1993
The Best Stage Scenes of 1994
The Best Stage Scenes of 1995
Monologues from Classic Plays 468 B.C. to 1960 A.D.
Scenes from Classic Plays 468 B.C. to 1970 A.D.
100 Great Monologues from the Renaissance Theatre
100 Great Monologues from the Neo-Classical Theatre
100 Great Monologues from the 19th C. Romantic & Realistic Theatre

Smith and Kraus *Books For Actors*
THE MONOLOGUE SERIES
The Best Men's / Women's Stage Monologues of 1994
The Best Men's / Women's Stage Monologues of 1993
The Best Men's / Women's Stage Monologues of 1992
The Best Men's / Women's Stage Monologues of 1991
The Best Men's / Women's Stage Monologues of 1990
One Hundred Men's / Women's Stage Monologues from the 1980's
2 Minutes and Under: Character Monologues for Actors
Street Talk: Character Monologues for Actors
Uptown: Character Monologues for Actors
Ice Babies in Oz: Character Monologues for Actors
Monologues from Contemporary Literature: Volume I
Monologues from Classic Plays
100 Great Monologues from the Renaissance Theatre
100 Great Monologues from the Neo-Classical Theatre
100 Great Monologues from the 19th C. Romantic and Realistic Theatres
A Brave and Violent Theatre: 20th C. Irish Monologues, Scenes & Hist. Context
Kiss and Tell: Restoration Monologues, Scenes and Historical Context
The Great Monologues from the Humana Festival
The Great Monologues from the EST Marathon
The Great Monologues from the Women's Project
The Great Monologues from the Mark Taper Forum
YOUNG ACTOR SERIES
Great Scenes and Monologues for Children
Great Monologues for Young Actors
Multicultural Monologues for Young Actors
SCENE STUDY SERIES
Scenes From Classic Plays 468 B.C. to 1960 A.D.
The Best Stage Scenes of 1995
The Best Stage Scenes of 1994
The Best Stage Scenes of 1993
The Best Stage Scenes of 1992
The Best Stage Scenes for Men / Women from the 1980's

If you require pre-publication information about upcoming Smith and Kraus books, you may receive our semi-annual catalogue, free of charge, by sending your name and address to *Smith and Kraus Catalogue, P.O. Box 127, One Main Street, Lyme, NH 03768. Or call us at (800) 895-4331, fax (603) 795-4427.*

The Best
Men's Stage Monologues
# of 1995

edited by Jocelyn A. Beard

The Monologue Audition Series

SK
A Smith and Kraus Book

Published by Smith and Kraus, Inc.
One Main Street, Lyme, NH 03768

First Edition: March 1996
10 9 8 7 6 5 4 3 2 1

The Monologue Audition Series ISSN 1067-134X

NOTE: These monologues are intended to be used for audition and class study; permission is not required to use the material for those purposes. However, if there is a paid performance of any of the monologues included in this book, please refer to the permissions acknowledgment pages to locate the source who can grant permission for public performance.

Contents

Preface, Jocelyn A. Beard vii

Introduction, Richard Brestoff ix

Barking Sharks, Israel Horovitz 1

Beast on the Moon, Richard Kalinoski (2) 2

Blink of an Eye, Jeremy Dobrish (2) 5

bliss, Benjamin Bettenbender (2) 7

By the Sea: Dusk, Terrence McNally (2) 11

A Candle in the Window, Tom Gilroy 13

Cannibal Cheerleaders on Crack, Billy Bermingham 14

A Cheever Evening, A.R. Gurney 16

Company Policy, Michael Ajakwe Jr. 18

Conversations with the Pool Boy, Robert Coles 19

Crow, Louis Nowra (2) 20

A Dead Man's Apartment, Edward Allan Baker 24

Dog Eat Dog, Karen Smith Vastola 25

Dog Opera, Constance Congdon 27

Emma's Child, Kristine Thatcher (2) 28

Every Seventeen Minutes the Crowd Goes Wild!, Paul Zindel 31

Gunplay, Frank Higgins 32

Half-Court, Brian Silberman (2) 34

Him, Christopher Walken 38

Kept Men, Richard Lay (2) 40

Metamorphoses, Michael Winn 42

Middle-Aged White Guys, Jane Martin 46

The Midnight Hour, James Campbell 47

My Virginia, Darci Picoult 48

New England, Richard Nelson 50

The Only Thing Worse You Could Have Told Me, Dan Butler 51

Phaedra, Elizabeth Egloff 54

The Professional, Dusan Kovacevic, tr. by Bob Djurdjevic (2) 57

The Psychic Life of Savages, Amy Freed (2) 60

Rain, Garry Williams 62

Safe House, WM. Seebring 64

Sanctuary, David Williamson 65

Self-Defense, Michael P. Scasserra 68

Sophistry, Jonathan Marc Sherman 72

Sugar Down Billie Hoak, Brian Silberman 73

Talk/Show, Michael P. Scasserra 75

The Ties that Bind, Regina Taylor (2) 78

Tough Choices for the New Century, Jane Anderson 80

Water and Wine, Stuart Spencer 81

Watbanaland, Doug Wright 82

Permission Acknowledgments 83

Preface

If I had to select one word or concept which I felt best described the 1995 theatrical season it would have to be "struggle." This season has offered many challenging roles for men which illustrate the global and domestic upheavals of the 1990's. Dusan Kovacevic's *The Professional* presents us with two former enemies struggling to find meaning in their new lives in a Belgrade no longer in the grip of communism. *Kept Men* by Richard Lay introduces us to a group of newly unemployed men who struggle to maintain what status quo they are able after falling victim to corporate downsizing. In Constance Congdon's tragic *Dog Opera*, we meet a man struggling to find love and survival in a world ravaged by disease. Brian Silberman presents the poignant struggle of two boys to survive on the streets in *Sugar Down Billie Hoak*. And in Tom Gilroy's *A Candle in the Window*, a young vet struggles to understand his sexuality.

Men struggling to triumph, men struggling to discover truth and men struggling just to survive. You will discover these themes again and again as you go through this book. The playwrights of 1995 have given remarkable voice to the process of conflict, and this process is essential to the continued evolution of theatre. 1995 has proved to be a theatrical watershed in what has so far been a very wild ride.

Please, read these plays for they are important works.

Break a leg!

Jocelyn Beard
Patterson, NY
Winter 1996

To my fabulous husband, Kevin Kitowski, whose on-going monologue is one of which I never tire.

Introduction

You fall in love. And as time goes by, you fight, make up, try again, give up, move on, come back. The push/pull of it all is exhilarating, exhausting, frustrating and rewarding.

No, we're not talking about women here, we're talking about our relationship with a monologue. Let's face it, a monologue *is* a relationship and our life with it goes through many stages (pun intended). If you're holding this book right now, chances are you're searching for audition pieces. And finding ones that you can have a relationship with is not easy. You must dance many of them across the floor before you settle down. So take your time. Play the field. Give everybody a whirl.

Luckily, this 1995 collection contains some of the best dancing partners around. The pieces range from a salesman whose product is Death, to a "piece of the universe's primordial ooze." You will be moved and astonished by playwrights as well known as Terrence McNally, Israel Horovitz, Jane Martin, and A.R. Gurney. And you will discover delightful treasures by writers whose names are, as yet, unfamiliar.

How is one to approach the wonders to be found in this volume? First, read them all. Don't worry if your age doesn't correspond to the character's. Read the monologue anyway. If it affects you strongly, go ahead and try it on. If the character is a boxer, don't pass it up just because you're out of shape. Read through it. You may discover that the power of the part does not lie in biceps or stomach muscles. If the piece is set in 1506, don't run because you think the writing will be obtusely stylized. Read through it. You may be swept away.

After you've read all the monologues, some will stand out. They will ask you for your voice, your body, your understanding and your passion. Heed the call. Go back and give them some time. Look more closely at them.

A monologue is a scene with a silent partner, and on your second look, you must determine who that partner is. Who is the monologue directed at? What is your character's relationship with that silent partner? Once you know that, another very important question presents itself. Why are you now telling this partner the things you are? The answer to this question is crucial. It will lead you to the point of the piece. Its reason for existence. Does your character want to *hurt* the silent other, does your character want the *relief* that confession brings, does your character want to *warn* the silent partner away from some danger, is your character selling something? What circumstances led the character to reveal these things *now*? These questions lead you out beyond the pieces themselves.

Find the plays. Monologues are excerpts from longer dramatic pieces and it is to them that you must ultimately refer. If you like a woman enough, you meet her family. If you like a monologue enough, you read the play. Remember, these marvels of theatrical writing have been severed from their roots, and for you to perform them with the confidence of full knowledge, you will need to put them back into their contexts. Then after reading the play, you will need to make some decisions.

The truth is, monologues are performed *out* of context. So actors sometimes need to make adjustments. If the character is Australian, and your dialect is not the best, and the basic nature of the piece is not destroyed by removing its "Austalian-ness," go ahead and try it in your natural voice. The piece may be effective for you even though you have partly altered it. But be careful. The fewer adjustments you make, the better.

As you set out on the wonderful, frustrating journey of making a monologue your own, take a moment to give thanks to the many gifted writers whose treasures you hold in your hands.

Go ahead. Fall in love. It's worth it.

Richard Brestoff
Actor and Author of *The Camera Smart Actor* and *The Great Acting Teachers and their Methods*

Barking Sharks
Israel Horovitz

RALPH BURKE: 60s, good-looking successful corporate executive
SCENE: New York City, present

Ralph is with his advertising agency representative, enjoying a successful new product introduction macho-style, when he suddenly reveals the truth of his existence.

○   ○   ○

RALPH BURKE: *Nothing* gives me pleasure. My first wife's dead. My second wife's re-married. None of my kids give a damn about me. They probably do, on some level. I mean, they probably talk about me in their psychoanalytic sessions, right? But, they don't ever, like, *call me*…I mean, they don't actually wanna *see me.* And, to tell you the God's honest truth, I don't really know, deep down, if I actually wanna see *them!* It's a terrible thing to say out loud, isn't it? I know, at my age, you're s'posed ta love takin' walks with your grandchildren, but, I don't, I really don't! I know they're just kids, and I should be generous with them and all, but, honest ta God, they're not nice people.

[EDDIE: Your *grandchildren?*]

RALPH BURKE: My whole *family.* Selfish, money-grubbing, nasty to each other, whiney, endless bickering…My son's a lousy husband and father, big-time. He's screwing anything that wears a skirt.

[EDDIE: He told you this?]

RALPH BURKE: It's obvious! I know what he's doin', 'cause he learned it from *me!* He acts like a piece of shit to his kids, and it makes me *hate myself!* *(Burke's emotions are over the top. He grabs a presentation notebook from the tabletop and flings it down on the floor, angrily.)*

Beast on the Moon
Richard Kalinoski

VINCENT: 16, orphan
SCENE: Milwaukee, WI 1920s

Vincent recounts a traumatizing incident at the orphanage to a sympathetic Seta.

○   ○   ○

VINCENT: *(Shuddering.)* Fath—Fath—Father Lewinski—I'm inna bathtub and he comes in there with that big cross he's got bouncing around and he don't say nothing, jus' gets a big teethy smile and a giggle and then he tries to yank me outta da tub…so so so I'm bangin' around tryin' to get out and he's grabbin' me but I'm slippery from the soap so I dodged outta der, and he don't want me naked all over da place, so he throws my clothes at me. I don't want no more shame…I don't want no more shame, Missus Tomasin. No more. I gotta mutha inna institution, I gotta father dead, ya know…I never screamed er cried er nuthin'…till now…till now.

Beast on the Moon
Richard Kalinoski

ARAM TOMASIAN: 30s-40s
SCENE: Milwaukee, WI 1920s

Aram, orphaned as a child, finally explains to his barren wife his obsession to have children.

O   O   O

ARAM: You don't know. You don't know me, Mrs. Tomasian. I talk! I talk all day! I am liked. All my customers, I treat them with respect. I give them their families…I am paid to make their children beautiful! *(Long pause.)* When they see their pictures they smile, because they see their children. Their beautiful children…and everyday I see their children…I see…their beautiful children. *(He is frightened.)*…the Italians, the Poles, they have so many— seven, eight children. Four sons, five sons…everyday I look at these beautiful children—and do you ever think of that, Seta, do you? Do you ever think of me there everyday looking at families I don't have? You tell me, Mrs. Tomasian, do you?

[SETA: *(Quietly.)* No.]

ARAM: *(Looking at the portrait.)* So this is my hope. Hope in a picture.

[SETA: I didn't know.]

ARAM: *(Trying to continue.)* I did it…I cut the holes…for hope…My father was lucky. He had a family. *(Pause.)* He made a place for me to hide—they put a hole in the floor, and I was to hide under my father's old coat. They told me to go there if anything happened and they stacked old blankets on top. In the night I heard the guns of the Turks. I slid underneath. There were shouts and shots and screaming—they poked at the pile of the blankets. The Turks were clumsy or lazy or drunk. They didn't find me. I lay for a long time, shivering…under my father's coat. When I came out, I was all wet, with urine, and sweat…there was blood…on the floor and the walls…on the ceilings, in the air. Oh, I ran into the backyard…outside…anywhere I thought, and then I saw…My mother had a line outside, for her wash, the Turks they had hung…they had hung…the heads of my family on the clothes…the

3

clothesline. The heads of my family, in my backyard, next to my mother's wash.

[SETA: *(Softly.)* Yes.]

ARAM: Later, inside the lining of the coat I found the picture—and I carried the coat with me in a sack. I went with the neighbors and they made me dress like a girl. I was a skinny girl for a long time. Just a skinny girl. As a girl I was very ugly. In the lining of the coat—my father had left me some rare stamps—his collection. And later, I bribed some Arabs with one of them, and then, later, bribed myself all the way to America…and bought a camera. I sat alone one night and made a new family picture, and wept to see them…coming alive in the chemicals, coming alive, Seta. Nineteen years old. I sat alone and looked at the picture coming alive in the chemicals and I took out a knife and cut out the heads of my father, Toros, my mother, Vartuhy, my little sister, Karin, and my brother Dickran…I cut out the heads of my family. I thought I could replace them. I really thought that's the way it would be. *(He clutches it.)* I thought…a wife…children…then I would forget. Completely. But I never forget. I never do.

Blink Of An Eye
Jeremy Dobrish

ANNOUNCER: any age
SCENE: New York City

Following an appearance by the one and only Julius Caesar, the Mephistophelean Announcer does his best to peddle life's ultimate commodity: death.

O   O   O

ANNOUNCER: Alright…, Mr. Julius Caesar everyone *(The sound of applause as Caesar exits.)* Now see, he was apprehensive at first. But eventually he came around. He took death home to see how he liked it and became one of our most satisfied customers. Now, I know you've heard the hype. The floating above your body, seeing the tunnel, seeing the light, hearing the voice. Well new and improved death will take you one step further. All the way home to your own personalized demise where you will discover your true self. You and your true self will spend eternity together and you will learn who you really are and what your destiny was. It's a beautiful feeling folks. No hell. No worms nibbling away at your body. There are so many misconceptions out there that give our product a bad name. Death can be fun.
(Simone enters., does tricks, tries to entertain, and so forth.)
ANNOUNCER: Does death look like this? *(A slide of the Grim Reaper. The sound of the "studio audience" saying "no".)* Does death look like this? *(A slide of the devil. The sound of the studio audience saying "no".)* Does death look like this? *(A slide of Boswell's face. The sound of the studio audience saying "maybe".)* Very good. Now remember death comes with a full lifetime warranty. No, that's a joke. But if you call today we will send you the complete death instructional home video as well as an autographed copy of "Standing Tall: the Rise and Rise of Patrick Ewing". And remember folks, death is not sold in any stores so do yourself a favor, and call today. *(The lights fade out on the Announcer and up on the Narrator.)*

Blink of an Eye
Jeremy Dobrish

MATTHEW: a homicidal maniac, 30-40
SCENE: New York City

Matthew, a triplet, has escaped from a mental institution with the intention of tracking down and killing his two brothers in a misguided effort to integrate his hopelessly divided personality. Here, he introduces himself.

○   ○   ○

MATTHEW: I am Matthew Farquar and I am loony-tunes. A bad-mama-jama. Stay out of my way, oh boy, or I will do something only a crazy man would do. Because I have nothing to lose. I am dark, evil, and sick. I'm the dissected frog in your locker, the car wreck you strain your head to see, and the pimple on the end of your nose. I am the piss in your soup, the pebble in your shoe, and the addiction that haunts you late at night. I'm your thumb slammed in a door, a kick in the stomach, and the pus in your wound. I am the headache that will not go away. *(He stops a moment to bite something off his thumbnail.)* I'm a missed freethrow, a sacked quarterback, and strike three in the bottom of the ninth. I'm a bad marriage, a clubbed seal, and the nerve ending at the root of your tooth. I am nails scratching across the blackboard, baby, ha-ha-ha. I'm the shadow that follows you, the bump in the night, and the monster under your bed. I am hell on earth, a living nightmare, and the sweat on your sheets. I am fear, loathing and hatred. I'm the bully after school, lard ass! I am sickness, rot, and decay. I'm a premature ejaculation, a faked orgasm, and your lover's deceitful secret. I am white noise, black rain, and dead skin. *(Pause.)* So…anyone want to get a drink with me after the show? *(Blackout. The sound of a Grandfather clock striking ten a little too quickly. The lights reveal Boswell following Matthew as he walks a pattern across the stage. Slide: "Et Tu Brute?".)*

bliss
Benjamin Bettenbender

CHICK: a man poised to kill, 30s
SCENE: Here and now

Chick has been hired by Jo-Lynne to kill Curtis, the man who killed her husband. Here, Chick rushes into Curtis's home and makes his intention clear.

○   ○   ○

CHICK: Check the bag first. *(Pause.)*
(Curtis rises up on one arm, moving painfully. He starts to get up but Chick springs off the chair and grabs the bag from the floor.)
CHICK: That's OK, I'll get it for you. *(He unzips the bag and removes a sawed-off twelve-gauge shotgun. He tosses the bag aside and walks towards Curtis, the shotgun leveled at his face.)* Well look at this! Seems you were within a cunt-hair of holding this bad boy in your hot little hands, huh, Curtis? Seems I was taking a hell of a chance playing around with you at the door like that. One slip and this metal was yours. I'd be standing there with my thumb up my ass trying to explain what this was all about, right? You holding this fucker in my face and me sweating like a pig. Damn! Whatever was I thinking.
(Curtis has backed up a few steps and stopped. Chick stands a moment watching him.)
CHICK: I guess I'm a little out of control. Running on autopilot or something, right? 'Cause I got to tell you, for the life of me I was planning on popping you the second you answered the door. Like, hello? BAM! It's fucking done. You know why? 'Cause I was kind of worried about you, Curtis. Well, not worried exactly. *(Pause.)* Scared shitless. I was scared shitless by you. I mean, you sounded like no one to fuck with, you know? I'm out in the car for the last twenty minutes talking myself into just walking up here. Saying, hey, he doesn't know you're coming. Just do it, right? Just get it done. You'll have the sawed-off in your hand, what can he do? *What* can the man *do?* And the next thing I know, I'm laying on the bell with the bag closed! No plan, no idea what I'm fucking doing there. I'm just waiting for you to answer

while I'm working on this line about being with a collection agency. *(He laughs.)* Like I said. Autopilot, right? *(Pause.)* I wonder what it means. *(Pause.)* You ever wonder about shit like that? You do something and you don't know why, but it's like some part of you knows exactly what it's doing so you say fine, go with it, knock yourself out. You know what I'm talking about? *(He stares at Curtis.)*

(Curtis doesn't respond.)

CHICK: Maybe what it means is, even though I felt scared, I really wasn't. Like it was just nerves, but I thought it was fear. Or maybe it was fear, but some part of me just decided to blow it off and go crazy. Like it was saying "fuck you" to me, "we're not blowing this just 'cause you're turning pussy on me." *(Pause.)* It's hard to say. 'Cause like I said, I was nervous about this, you being mister one-punch and all. Like Bruce Lee in real life or something. And there's me handing this bag over like I'm some badass who doesn't have to worry about shit. *(He stares at Curtis.)* You think that's it? You think maybe I'm a badass and I don't know it? You think that's what my autopilot's saying? *(Pause.)* Well shit, let's find out. *(Chick walks to within a few feet of Curtis. He slowly extends his right arm until the shotgun is only inches from Curtis's face. They stand that way a moment, unmoving.)* Your move, champ. You're as fast as I think you are, now's the time to show it.

(Curtis continues to stand. Chick edges forward a bit so that the barrel is barely touching Curtis's forehead.)

CHICK: One second and it's over. *(Pause.)* One second. *(Pause. Chick then slowly moves backwards. He lowers the shotgun to his side. He then turns and spins around wildly.)* Oooooooooooo-hoo! Goddamn, that was hot! That was a serious fucking rush, am I right?! My arm's tingling like…I don't know. Just tingling. You don't have any beer, do you?

(Curtis stares at him.)

CHICK: Hello?

bliss
Benjamin Bettenbender

CHICK: a man poised to kill, 30s
SCENE: Here and now

Chick, who has killed once before, here explains why it's important to give his intended victim an opportunity to beg for his life.

O   O   O

CHICK: Well then we'll just have to slow it down so that you *can* follow it. I'm working in a laundromat a few years back, I'm doing my job—which is basically just sitting there all day to make sure no one walks out with one of the dryers—I'm doing my job and minding my own fucking business, and this guy who owns the place shows up every couple of days just to look around and act like a big-dick in his fucking store. Course the only way he can do that is to piss on me every chance he gets, telling me I don't do shit, telling me I'm lazy, I'm stupid, I'm stealing from him, I'm lucky to even have a job. So finally I say, fine, I'm such an asshole? I'll do you a favor and leave. Pay me for the week and I'm out of here. So this guy goes ape-shit on me. Starts telling me what a worthless piece of shit I am, how I'm a waste of air space, how there's not a single thing about me that justifies me being alive, and I say, Whoa! Who are you to be talking about what's worth keeping someone alive, and he starts screaming about name something! Name one fucking thing you do or you are that is worth living for! Name *one goddamned thing!* Name it!, leaning in real close to me so I can smell his dog-shit breath and see the spit flying out of his mouth. Name it! So I tell him sorry, it's not my problem. It's his. Just pay me my money and get out of my face. And he takes out this roll and peels off some cash and throws it in front of me like he thinks I won't pick it up, but I just pocket it real sweet and smile and say, "hey, no hard feelings." And I'm out of there. *(Pause.)* Took four days, but I finally got him standing there one night locking up the store with no car parked in front of it, just a clear shot from the street to the curb to his fat ass playing with his key ring. And I pull out of the driveway I'm waiting in and floor the fucker and swerve just right and…BAPP! He's through the glass and headfirst onto a folding table. And I get out of the car, and I walk through the hole used to be the door, and I stare at this guy thinking who's worthless now, motherfucker, when it hits me. It was like a sick feeling in my stomach and this dizzy spell all at once, and I'm going, oh shit! Oh shit oh shit oh shit! I should've asked him first. I should've asked him what he was asking me. Asked him to name it. Name it why I shouldn't fucking kill him. Name it what justified him being alive. Him staying alive. Name it for me now. *(Pause. Chick moves away a moment, lights a cigarette, then turns back to face Curtis.)* They knew goddamned well I did the guy on purpose, but my blood alcohol was high from me sipping wine in the car, and my public defender was all over 'em about my old Le Mans being totaled and no way I would've risked getting killed myself if I was trying to commit murder, right? He said I was just driving up onto the sidewalk to yell at the guy and lost control of the car. Simple. So the State took the sure shot and offered manslaughter and ten and I'm in Rahway doing two with good behavior, which may not seem like a lot, but being white and a hit-and-run pussy, you catch a lot more shit than most, which still would've been OK except some asshole poking around records found out my real name wasn't Chico like I was telling 'em, it was Chick. *(Pause.)* Chick. *(Pause.)* If I'd a walked in there with the words "fuck me" tattooed across my lips, it could not have been worse. But even with all of that, with all the shit I had to eat 'cause of it, it would've still been worth it if I could've just asked the man that question. Asked him to name it for me. Name it so I could know what makes someone *deserve* to live. I thought about that…a lot. All the fucking time. *(Pause. He stares at Curtis.)* But now I get another chance. Now I get to prove my theory once and for all. You tell me in one shot why you should live and I'll listen with an open mind. You convince me, then you're free and I'm a better man for it. Shit, I'm likely to kiss your feet and crawl out the front door backwards. You don't? Then you die, and I walk out of here knowing that if I am wasting air space, at least I got a lot of company. Either way, I can rest easy at night knowing I got the answer. Shit, the very worst that could happen is I end up back inside, only this time I got a righteous, bona fide murder conviction I can hang on my wall so maybe I'm the one looking down on some bobbing scalp for a change. So if you're all clear now on what the fuck I'm asking you, you might want to get started 'cause the clock is ticking.

By the Sea: Dusk
Terrence McNally

WILLY: jogger at the beach
SCENE: Dusk

Willy tries to talk to swimmer, Marsha—she rejects him—he responds.

O   O   O

WILLY: You're not my type anyway. You can die with your secret, bitch. *(To audience.)* I hate women like that, don't you? I hate people like that, period. I mean, what's the big deal in talking to one another? Everybody's got some goddamn hidden agenda you're supposed to figure out. Life's too short. You are looking at a man without an agenda. What you see in Willy Osowski is what you get in Willy Osowski. That's me, in case you hadn't guessed. I'm Willy Osowski. We're not talking about somebody else here. We're talking about yours truly. Where was I? Concentration is not my strong point. Making love is. That was a joke. My sense of humor is. That was another joke. I'll stop making jokes. Just give me a second. I remember! We were talking about how what you see in me is what you get in me. I run about this deep. No, about this deep. That doesn't mean I'm shallow. I'm like clear Caribbean water you can see right to the bottom of, even at thirty feet. It just looks like it's shallow, but when you try to dive down to the bottom of it for the sunken treasure, Spanish gold or caskets of jewels you heard or hoped were waiting for you there, you think your lungs are going to explode before you get there. Sometimes you can't do it and you have to shoot back up to the surface for another gulp of air before you can try again. You want my advice? Take it easy. Take a real, real deep breath this time. What's your hurry? I'm worth the effort. I'm that piece of Spanish gold, that pirates' treasure, that king's ransom you've been looking for all your life. I'm right here. A good man is hard to find. I'm a good man. You've found him.

By the Sea: Dusk
Terrence McNally

WILLY: jogger at the beach
SCENE: Dusk

Willy having met Dana, a jogger, and Marsha, a swimmer on beach, at dusk, tries to impress them with this obviously tall tale.

O   O   O

WILLY: I made really spectacular love with a beautiful young woman who clearly was as physically and emotionally eager for some kind of one-on-one contact as I was. It was amazing. I saw her coming toward me across the parking lot. I'd just gotten off my bicycle. She had on shorts that were slit up the side, so I could tell that she was tan all over, which meant that she sun-bathed in the nude, like I do, and when she got up close to me she ripped my shirt open and started playing with my chest and I ripped her blouse open and started burying my face in her beautiful, beautiful breasts and before I knew it she had my pants down around my ankles and I pulled her shorts and panties down while she wrapped her legs around my waist and then we fell back on the hood of a car and the combination of the warm metal and her soft, soft flesh and my hard, hard muscle and what we were doing on that hot, hot car hood produced an almost instantaneous climax for both of us and before you knew it we both collapsed on the hood in happy exhaustion and agreed we didn't care if anyone saw us like this, including the town police or my wife or her husband, we were both so happy, so spent, it would be worth it.

A Candle in the Window
Tom Gilroy

JOHN: an ex-marine, inarticulate and occasionally violent, 27
SCENE: The suburban northeast

A veteran of the Gulf War, macho John, has been tortured by the possibility that he may have slept with Nathan, his best friend, while they served in the Marines. A few years and a broken marriage later, John allows himself to be picked up by Maddy, a pragmatic woman he meets at a bar. When their lovemaking goes awry, Maddy is able to coax the story of his night with Nathan from him, beginning with the following description of the night he first met his wife.

JOHN: I had never seen anything like this. I mean. I lived in suburban Pennsylvania, you know. And here's these guys eating cookies off of these squirming girls, and they were liking it! American college girls! Because they wanted to! And I was just laughing, and Debbie came up to me and started talking to me. I didn't know what to say. She knew we were Marines by our tattoos, and I couldn't believe with all the college guys in there she was talking to *me*. I mean, I was looking just to find some girl who was totally drunk and I could just screw and maybe stretch it out for the week, or screw some of her friends or whatever—nothing heavy. And instead I met this girl who I really liked. And she was like out of an underwear catalog. And we started talking and I looked in her eyes and she was beautiful and she told me not everyone could take the Marines. And I knew right then I had waited my whole life for this to happen. I couldn't believe she didn't have some guy who was better looking, or richer, or smarter, or whatever. And I realized the Marines had elevated me to a level I never would have reached on my own. The American Dream. And I said to myself "Don't ever fuck this up. The Marines got you here. Work hard. Stay on this path and you get everything." And I was going to follow the plan forever.

[MADDY: What happened? *(A pause.)*]

JOHN: *(awkward)* Well, I fucked up. I made a mistake and when you make a mistake you can't go back and change it.

Cannibal Cheerleaders on Crack
Billy Bermingham

THINGAMAJIG: a piece of the universe's primordial goo visiting earth in the form of a human being, 20-30

SCENE: Washington, DC, sooner than you think

Thingamajig has transformed himself into a human for the express purpose of delivering a warning to the leaders of the planet. The pattern of ecological destruction must be halted, or the earth will be destroyed. Unfortunately, Thingamajig's mission is soon forgotten as he gets sucked deeper and deeper into the ennui of human life. Here, the poor lost creature struggles to remember his purpose.

(Thingamajig has his jumpsuit on backwards and sports a yellow ear-tag. He's very frazzled. He is under a solo spot.)

THINGAMAJIG: I had something to do. Something important. I can't remember. Can't think. And I can't remember what I believe in. Everything is connected with invisible whispers of guilt and profit so I can't distinguish yes from no or right from wrong. I can't remember what's okay, what I can have; I can't have tuna sandwiches anymore because of the depletion of the Rain Forest, and my hamburgers support Death Squads, and my Government imports all the *good* drugs but I can't have them or they'll take away my car and my house which is killing the *something*—so maybe I'm better off without it. And I can't remember how to speak anymore because our language is dead…because there are no more adjectives anymore, everything is *like* and *Y'Know* and *Fucking* this and *Fucking* that but I can only say that word at the *top of my lungs in public* not when people pay good money to hear it or they'll take away·my house which is killing the *something* so maybe I'm better off without it, and they'll take away my BMW and my CD and my TV and my VCR and my *killer hamburgers* and all the other *shit* they said was good when I was growing up and I believed them but they *lied* but they convinced themselves they weren't really lying so—did they lie? So I don't know who to believe in anymore. I don't believe in God—except when I really need him because then when he doesn't help me I can say *good, I was right* or *He was probably too busy pulling the wings off some bug!* But it doesn't matter anyway because after they've taken away all my shit they'll tell me it was all for my own good and then they'll beat me down and kick me 'til all my bloody dreams and broken promises spill out onto the floor so the man in charge can check his reflection and slick back his hair in the puddle of my wasted life. And they'll take away my clothes and my dignity and my identify and they'll scrub me down and tell me everything's okay now, that *I don't have to make any more decisions*—that they'll do it for me—and they'll put me in a warm soft place and I'll sleep.

A Cheever Evening

A.R. Gurney

ETHAN: a man whose wife has just left him, again, 40s
SCENE: America in the 50s and 60s

Here, Ethan describes a series of nocturnal visits by a prowler that culminate in an interesting discovery.

ETHAN: *(To audience.)* It's late at night. I'm reading *Anna Karenina*. My wife Rachel is up in Seal Harbor with the kids, while I've stayed down here to work. Our living room is comfortable, the book is interesting, and the neighborhood is quiet, what with so many people away. *(He reads, then puts down his book.)* Oh hell, I might as well admit it. Rachel's left me. She's left me twice before, but this is it. Hey, that's OK! You can cure yourself of a romantic, carnal, and disastrous marriage. But like any addict in the throes of a cure, you have to be careful of every step you take. *(The telephone rings.)* Like not answering the telephone. *(Indicating the phone.)* Because that's Rachel. Maybe she's repented, or wants to tell me it's rained for five days, or one of the children has a passing fever—something…*(Shouting at phone.)* But I will not be tempted to resume a relationship that has been so miserable! *(The phone stops, he resumes reading. Cricket sounds. Then a dog barks.)* That's the Barstow's dog. He barks endlessly. *(The barking stops.)* That's funny. Why did he stop?
(He listens. A shadowy figure, in raincoat and hat, enters stealthily upstage. He is played by the third actor.)
ETHAN: Then I hear very close outside, a footstep and a cough.
(The figure coughs.)
ETHAN: I feel my flesh get hard—you know that feeling—and know I am being watched from the picture window. *(He jumps up.)*
(The figure goes.)
ETHAN: I flip on the outside carriage light, and look out. But now the lawn is empty. *(Returns to his chair.)* The next night, I leave the outside light on, settle in with my book, and hear the dog bark once again.

(Barking; the figure appears downstage.)

ETHAN: And there he is again! Now in the window above the piano . . . *(He yells.)* Hey, you! Get the hell out of here! *(He grabs the phone, dials "0.")*
(The figure disappears.)

ETHAN: Rachel is gone! There's nothing to see!…Oh excuse me, operator. Give me the police. *(Toward off stage.)* Leave me alone!…Police? Ah, is that you, Stanley? Stanley, I want to report a prowler!…What? *(To audience.)* He seems to think I am trying to undermine real estate values. *(To phone.)* Yes…All right. Good night, Stanley. *(To audience.)* He said he was underpaid and overworked, and that if I wanted a guard around my house, I should vote to enlarge the police force.

(Lights change to daylight. We hear a train announcement: "The eight-eighteen for Grand Central is arriving on track two." Ethan puts on his jacket, adjusts his tie, and grabs his briefcase. Herb Marston, played by third actor, comes on D.R, as if onto the station platform. He wears a hat and also carries a briefcase. He looks up the track, waiting for the train to arrive. Stepping onto the "platform" D.L.; to audience.)

ETHAN: The next day I see my man. He is waiting on the platform for the eight-eighteen. It's Herb Marston, who lives in the big yellow house on Glenhollow Road. *(Ethan goes up to him.)* Hey! I don't mind you looking in my windows, Mr. Marston, but I wish you wouldn't trample on my wife's begonias!

(Marston checks his watch as Ethan turns to audience.)

ETHAN: That's what I *planned* to say. But I didn't.

Company Policy
Michael Ajakwe Jr.

LANCE MALONE: a young man starting a new job
SCENE: Corporate offices

When his boss, a white woman, makes a sexual advance upon him, Lance does his best to turn her down. When she insists that she understands the pain that he must feel as a black man trapped in the white corporate world, he becomes furious and tells her exactly what he thinks.

O   O   O

LANCE: *(Shaking his head.)* No. *(Beat.)* I'm sick of you white women always trying to jump on the Black bandwagon of pain and suffering. It ain't the same. Any Black person whose grown up in this country will tell you that. It ain't the same. You think being a woman automatically qualifies you to be Black? Think again, Betsy Ross. It ain't the same. You're the baby-making machine of the knife that's been in my back for four centuries. So, ya see, Anne Marie, it ain't the same. Because no matter how low you sink on the social totem pole, you'll never sink as low as me because you are the mother of your bully. No matter how much he torments you, he will never truly harm his Maker, for to harm his Maker would be to harm himself. So unless you plan to stop making babies, I suggest you find some other miserable, less-crowded rollercoaster to ride on.

Conversations With The Pool Boy

Robert Coles

STU: a transplanted New Yorker now living in the Caribbean, 40s
SCENE: The US Virgin Islands, the present

When Arthur, a harried New Yorker comes for a visit, Stu is reminded of the state he was in when he first arrived in the Virgin Islands. He tells Arthur the tale of that first visit, and cautions his impatient friend that it will take three days for the process of unwinding to be complete.

O   O   O

STU: The first day I got here I made fun of everything. Jimmy had dragged me down here on vacation. I couldn't imagine a more insipid place to be—stuck on an island for two weeks with Jimmy—not a happy person though I'll admit I was stupid enough to more or less marry him—and 5000 straight couples drinking rum and doing the limbo 24 hours a day. Funny thing happened—after three days this incredible serenity came over me. I was able to ignore not only the straight people and their 17 different colors of cocktails which somehow turned placid insurance clerks from Topeka into Dionysian revelers, but also Jimmy, whose misery and dissatisfaction with everything from the paint color in our hotel room to the lack of suitably tropical foliage on the island spiraled into a frenzy of outrage at the injustice of life and the insensitivity of me. He of course employed the nuclear weapon—refusing to have sex with me. But it didn't matter. The *island* was making love to me. The look of it, the feel of it, the sound of it, the people—the real people, not the tourists. Yes, the *pace* of it. The *Caribbean* was caressing me—the water, the sun—and after making love to me, it didn't complain about the service at the hotel. So I decided, then and there: Fuck Jimmy, fuck my job, fuck New York, fuck *everything*. *This* is where I need to be. Six months later I was here—new job, no Jimmy. And I've never looked back. Three days. Three days was all it took. I give you three days, Arthur. After that, fuck you, too. You're welcome to remain in my home the full two weeks, but remember, it only costs $25 to change your ticket. I'll pay for it. Go back early. You want to stay crabby, stay crabby. You deserve New York, although I doubt the City will welcome you on your return. I'll give you Jimmy's number. Call him up and complain together. You'll both love it. I'll go get your room ready. Three days, Arthur.

Crow
Louis Nowra

Vince: a tent boxer, 20s
Scene: Darwin, Australia, 1942

The son of a racially mixed couple, Vince sadly belongs to neither's world. Instead, he travels the Outback as a tent boxer. Here, he describes a typical night of boxing matches to his mother and brother.

O   O   O

Vince: You'd love it. The tent and all.
[Boofhead: Yeh?]
Vince: Yeh. See, they pay their money, thinking, "I don't need to go three rounds, I can punch this Abo out in one." They get excited seeing me. This boom boom of the bass drum calling the audience in, *Bang! Bang!*, the spruiker outside the tent—*(Imitating a spruiker.)* 'Come in, see if you can go three rounds with the Ebony Prince—see if you can knock him down." They strip, looking like white grubs. They put on some gloves, thinking they're world champions. They come swinging, like some piece of corrugated iron flapping in a cyclone. All around me there is this sound—this roar and if you listen real careful you can hear what the crowd's shouting, "Kill the Abo!" The first times I wanted to kill the bastard. Christ, his defences open. Easy, easy as pie to take him in one punch.
(Both Boofhead and Crow are caught up in the story.)
[Boofhead: You knock him out in one punch?]
Vince: Nah—doesn't make a contest, doesn't make the tent show money. Boss doesn't like it. So you play with him. Make 'em think they're good. They swing away, hardly landing a punch and everyone's fooled, thinking I'm being beaten by some yahoo. Round one, he goes back into his corner. Cocky. His friend's slapping him on the back. "Give it to the boong next round." I jab at him in round two. Just on the shoulders, hitting his arm muscles. *(He demonstrates to Boofhead.)* Just there.
[Crow: It hurt him, right?]
[Boofhead: *(Exasperated with his mother.)* 'Course it does, mum.]

VINCE: His arms begin to feel like lead. He begins to understand, though his mates don't, that I am playing with him. I can take him out any time. In his eyes you see—he's got The Fear. Back on his stool at the end of round two, his mates are wiping him down, urging him on. "Go on, Ern, punch that black bastard out." The bell rings for round three and he comes toward me trying to look tough, but his gloves feel as heavy as medicine balls and he's afraid of what I am going to do to him, but he can't run because his mates would laugh at him. For the first time he's got The Fear of a blackfella. He swings and to the spectators they look like they're connecting. I jab him back, for every time he takes a swing at me. My punches look piss weak— but he'll have the bruises for weeks. He wants to fall down and get it over with, but his mates urge him on. He's like those cattle down at the abattoirs who, just before the whack behind their ears, know they're going to cop it and are stunned at what's about to happen. I throw a punch. It seems wild and a last gasp, a lucky punch, but it hits him where I want him to be hit. It's like a sledgehammer into his stomach. He gasps, like a tyre being punctured and I smell the terror and the booze pouring out of him. The crowd goes quiet seeing this white grub wriggling on the canvas. See, they think it was just a blackfella's lucky punch. They're all clammering to have a go at me. I make the Boss a fortune.

(Crow and Boofhead applaud.)

Crow
Louis Nowra

Vince: a tent boxer, 20s
Scene: Darwin, Australia, 1942

Vince has returned to Darwin to claim Ruth, the woman he loves. When he discovers that she is pregnant with another man's child, he flies into a rage. His passion nearly spent, Vince here confesses the agony of his life on the road.

○   ○   ○

Vince: I'm just a tent boxer, Ruthie. Just a tent boxer. When I left, I thought I could do it. You know, do a bit of tent boxing—be seen by some fella who'd think I was championship material. And this fella in Rockhampton did. A month in the tent show and I'm on my way—so long fellas! Cock of the hoop, cock of the walk. Did three professional fights. Each time, I've got him. Got him like a kangaroo in the spotlight. And I start in for the kill, but I get angry and wild, wanting to finish him off—I leave my guard open—I lose the fight, then the next three. Same thing—a rush of blood. I should have won them all. My manager gives up on me. I do the grog, I do the gambling and pretty soon I'm back in the tent show again, tail between my legs. I dream of getting back into pro, doing it right. But each night another town, another drink, another game of cards. Like, I can't stop myself. All the time I'm thinking of you—
[Ruth: Bullshit—]
Vince: The truth, Ruthie. The truth. I'd think of you, how good looking you are but I couldn't write. Didn't have the right words. Then one month I saved, saved up heaps. It wasn't like pockets of gold but it was enough, you know. I was in Cairns and thought to myself if I stick with the troupe I'm gonna spend it, so I think I'll hitchhike back to Darwin, back to you. First ride I didn't get far and I was stranded in some town miles from anywhere. I wait for a lift, I drink a bit, try out my luck with cards. Couple of days later, I get another lift. Another town. I do the same thing. I don't know why. I don't want to, but I do. All the time I want to come home to you. It goes on and on. I ask one driver to drop me off in between towns. He thinks I'm looney

but I think, "There'll be no temptation out there," and I walk through the red dust, through the rain and I feel low. I hitchhike my way to the next town and I gamble more and my stake gets smaller and smaller. I can't even explain to myself, Ruthie: I love you, I want to come home with money and I lose it, like I got some demon inside me saying, "Spend it, Vince, spend it", and I do. All of it. 'Til, finally, I hock me gloves. That's all I got left and I hock 'em. Fifty miles outside of Darwin I got nothing. Nothing. Can't even tell you I'm making it as a pro boxer. I sit down on the side of the road and I think to myself, don't go to Darwin, turn around and go back—she won't want you. Then I think, make this your last gamble, Vince. First car or truck that stops, wherever it's going, I'm gonna take it. Sort of like gambling with God or fate, I guess. A cattle truck stops and it's going to Darwin. I think to myself: this is fate. It wants me to go to Darwin and to you. Now I think, Ruthie, that the driver was the devil.

A Dead Man's Apartment

Edward Allan Baker

LONNIE: 38
SCENE: Present, Summertime, apartment

Lonnie is having an affair with Nickie, Nickie's daughter, Valerie, is morose and claims to want out of life. Lonnie talks some of his style of common sense to her.

O O O

LONNIE: I don't know what to tell you…I got through it. We all get through it. You do what you have to do and you get through it an yeah yeah most of it sucks but you push on, push on past the beatin's and the bein ignored an push past no one there to hold you an you fuckin' push on past when you think you don't matta an nothin matters an there's no peace in anybody's fuckin' house! For Chrissakes people dyin for getting laid an other people dying cause they can't get laid an you kids…you Goddamn kids nowadays…you want all the answers like right away! "Gimme an answer or I'll kill myself!" *Well fuck you!* You don't think we had…we adults had pain when we was growin up?! For Chrissakes *wake the fuck up* an be thankful you got a roof over ya head an food on the table an a bed to wallow over your bullshit in! Be thankful for the malls you hang out in an for the stupid clothes ya wear an the teachers you insult and hate!
(Valerie gets up from the couch to cross the room and is stopped by Lonnie who spins her around to face him. He shakes her.) Just know that all this will pass, Goddamn it, all…of…this…will…pass!

Dog Eat Dog
Karen Smith Vastola

KIRT: 20s

Kirt relates a story of corporate privilege far removed from anything he had experienced before.

O   O   O

KIRT: In his private suite...Boy, these guys in white elephant corporations. They may brag at their stockholders meeting how they cut their work force by five percent and saved the bottom line, but that doesn't stop them from treating themselves like corporate pashas...We're sitting there shooting the shit, you know New York Knicks, O.J. trial, his golf game and I hear this chime. I mean a chime, not someone's voice screeching through the telephone intercom, but a regular chime. Not a ding-dong, but a wind chime, like you'd expect at the entrance of a...I don't know...a Japanese whore house. And then the sweetest, softest voice asks, *(imitates woman's voice)* "Mr. Tucker, may I send in the coffee now?" Not, do you want the coffee now? Or, excuse me, the coffee's ready. But, may I send the coffee in. Like he was some kind of delicate egg that would crack if she spoke too loudly. Tucker looks at me and gestures, "Ready," and I nod back "Sure." So he says, "Certainly" to the intercom which is so high tech that it picks up his reply from the other end of this major, major suite. And a couple minutes later, I hear a soft knock at the door and this woman, in a black waitressy kind of uniform pushes a cart through the door. Right away, Tucker shuts up as if this woman with the cart would overhear some vital information, like a company stock split. And I stop in mid-sentence about my theory that Marcia Clark and Johnny Cochoran have the hots for each other. And all I hear for a few seconds is the tinkle of silver and china as this woman tries to maneuver this cart, as quietly as possible across the floor. She finally reaches the place where we're sitting and Tucker gives her a *Father's Knows Best* Smile and says, "Hi, Betty, how's the family?" *(imitates Betty Rubble's voice)* "Oh fine, Mr. Tucker, just fine. Can I pour you some coffee?" "That'd be great," he says. It goes back and forth like this for a couple of minutes. She pours my coffee. The cart is loaded with bagels, cream cheese, pastries, fresh

25

strawberries, even whipped cream. It could be a school breakfast program at P.S. 104 for a week. So the woman starts to slowly push the cart back across the room and I'm sitting there thinking about how back at my office if I even ask a female employee to hand me the coffeepot after she's finished filling up her cup, I run the risk of being labeled a sexist pig and being slapped with a harassment suit. As I'm thinking about this, the door quietly closes and the woman leaves, and Tucker turns to me and says, "I don't know about that Clark bitch, but that Cochoran looks like the kind of black pimp that would screw anything that walks."

[WALTER: Wheee. What the hell did you say?]

Dog Opera
Constance Congdon

JACKIE: an ingenious street hooker, 17
SCENE: Here and now

Jackie has been working the streets for a year or so and in that time has managed to accumulate an amazing store of knowledge from watching educational TV in motel rooms.

O   O   O

JACKIE: Crickets make that sound by rubbing their parts together—they're trying to get a date of some kind. They're also eating spiders as they do this. It's a beautiful night.

Fireflies are mooning each other. They die in a few weeks. In the grass and trees, insect life is trying to overpopulate in between doing search and destroy attacks on each other. Once this whole state was a swamp and dinosaurs sloshed around. Now their decay could ignite a fire fifty-feet high. Trees died to make those houses. And under all of this is a layer of dead Indians. If motel rooms didn't have cable, wouldn't know any of this, and I'd be a lot happier. Everyone says I'm smart and I shoulda stayed in school. Well, yeah. Where would I have lived, I wonder? I have some skills—I can put on a condom with my teeth, before the guy even realized it's there.

Mostly, I jerk off to music of my choice. I take requests but I will not do "People" by Barbara Streisand or anything of a religious nature.

(Looking down the street.)

Here they come—on their way home from work, in their big damn cars with the ample backseats. But I won't be getting in even wrapped in latex. I have a date tonight. With somebody's husband—yours?

(Sees car pulling up.)

Oh my god. He brought the station wagon—with the kid's car seat still in the back. No graham cracker crumbs on this boy—we're getting a room!

(He waves to the driver and exits to get into the car.)

Emma's Child
Kristine Thatcher

HENRY FARRELL: 46
SCENE: Doctor's office

Jean, his wife, has asked Henry's blessing to care for and possibly adopt the severely retarded and sick infant who, if born healthy, would have been their adoptive son. Henry responds.

O　　　O　　　O

HENRY: My best judgment is that you have no *idea* what you're doing. *If* Robin survives, he'll languish his whole life, and I will watch you struggle to fulfill some kind of promise that no one in the world expects you to keep: not me, not our family, not our friends, not the agency, not even Emma. If he *dies*, we'll have another round of misery like we've had for the last month. And Jean? I don't know how you imagine you are capable to taking it. Even if you *can* take it, and believe me, I'm *not* thinking of you at the moment, I can't take it! Although you don't remember, I'm part of this. I'm the one who picks up the pieces. I'm the one who held you, and heard you, and fed you, and coaxed you to bed for nights on end…You've asked for my blessing? Well, you can't have it. You can't have it.

Emma's Child

Kristine Thatcher

SAM STORNANT: 40s
SCENE: Sitting in the woods in the rain

Sam remembers when he began to date Franny, and what fatherhood came to mean to him.

O   O   O

SAM: The kid ambushed her when she wasn't looking. Now, she's hooked. Same thing happened to me when I first met Tom. Franny and I had been going out for about three weeks before she introduced me to him. It was Easter Sunday. We'd gone to church, all three of us, and I was going to spring for a big breakfast. She said he liked waffles. We were walking toward the front door of Uncle John's Pancake House. I had just taken her hand, when the little shit, all of seven years old, suddenly raced between us, in a fucking rage. He screamed, "I break your love!" Then, he smashed his arm across our fingers, broke our hands apart, and burst into tears. Franny stooped to talk to him—she was twenty-two years old, and so God Almighty beautiful—I thought, "If I can win this jealous little bugger, I can win her." So that's what I decided to do. I bought him presents. I took him to amusement parks, and circuses. We went fishing, we went to basketball games. I'm the one who brought him home the Harley.

[HENRY: The Harley?]

SAM: Remember that night?

[HENRY: Vividly.]

SAM: If you're a parent, there's nothing worse, than when your teenager is not home yet, and the phone rings after midnight. They brought us to where he was. We sat next to his bed holding hands. She was thinking—whatever she was thinking, I never knew. But, I was thinking back to the day I first met him. All the bribes, all those years, were nothing but a plea to him to let me stay close to his mother. Until the night of the accident, honest to God, I never realized, it was the little bugger who had the hammerlock on me. I would have done anything, *any*thing to keep him alive. Scotch-tape him back together, I don't care. You know, I didn't have a thing to do with bring-

...ig that kid into this world, but, I was the only father he was ever going to know, and he, sure as hell, was my only son. I'd be goddamned if I was going to let him go without a fight. At the time I married her, everybody thought she was so lucky. I was this white knight, who'd made an honest woman of her at last, who had taken on the support of the bastard son; but that night in the hospital, looking down at him, I realized for the first time what I must have known all along; from that Easter morning on, he had been my little boy. I was the lucky one.

Every Seventeen Minutes the Crowd Goes Wild!

Paul Zindel

DAN: a teenager
SCENE: Here and now

Dan, along with his brothers and sister, has been abandoned by his parents and communicates with them by fax only. Here, he reflects on his mother.

O   O   O

DAN: The only thing I noticed different about my mother was the way she would sit around the house crying a lot—which, I suppose, is unusual for a psychotherapist. She seemed obsessed with the case history of this one child patient she had. She kept printing out copies of it and leaving it around our breakfast table and at the neighborhood ashrams and supermarkets. It was something horrible that had happened to a ten-year-old boy at Christmas. His parents were loaded. Filthy rich. The father was a Hollywood producer. His mother was a Mutual Funds feminist. And they wanted to surprise their son with the greatest Christmas ever—so they bought him wonderful things: a Schwinn 10-speed, rollerblades, a Lionel electric train set, skis, a sled, a tennis racket, a dog, candy, a BB pistol, a Swiss army knife—a Christmas tree flooded with gift-wrapped boxes and bows and tinsel everywhere. A huge living room crammed with presents and candy canes. They had created this dream for their son, and on Christmas morning, their son came down the stairs into the living room—this ten-year-old boy saw this fantasy they bought him—and he burst into tears! "What's the matter, son?" his father cried out, rushing to him, holding him, hugging him—"Is there something you had your heart set on that you don't see? Is there something we forgot?" And the kid, wailing through his tears said, "I don't know, but there *could* be. There *could* be!" And that was when his father took back his hand and slapped his son with all his might. He slapped him and slapped him and slapped him!

Gunplay
Frank Higgins

A Man: 30-40
Scene: Here and now

Here, a self-proclaimed ladies' man reveals his secret for scoring with dates.

○   ○   ○

(A man mimes lifting a dumbbell.)

MAN: So am I a stud? I guess. But it's got nothing to do with the size of my dick. I first noticed something wacky about women and sex in college. You can't believe how many girls fantasize about their professor. I bet every girl's thought about it, and a lot of 'em have acted on it. And the ones I talk to who did, they tell me when he unbuttoned her blouse and opened her bra, they were more turned on than they've ever been in their life. Why? Taboo. Danger.

Friend of mine's a cop. Took his new girlfriend with him on an off-duty stake-out. So they spot the guy he's waiting for, follow in the car. When it's over, guy takes his girl home to drop her off; she *tells* him to come in. She tears his clothes off.

Now we're not gonna win any prizes with women's libbers with this, but my point is, I'm telling the truth. And truth is scary. Truth doesn't have an ideology. Truth just *is*. And if you got the guts to speak the Truth, Truth gets you in trouble. Ask Galileo.

So what is the truth? Who have the women in this building dated? Guys like us. And most guys like us are boring. So, I'm on the first date; we have dinner. And early on I say that I need to drop by the shooting range. She's glad. I've got plans for later that night that don't include her, which means I'm not trying to talk her into bed. She asks me if I hunt; no. She likes that. White-collar women love wolves and whales. I say the range isn't far, why not come with me? She likes to think she's open-minded, she comes. I start with the round targets. And I always have at least two pieces. She puts in the ear plugs, stands near me; I use a nine millimeter like Mel Gibson…*(Or the movie star of the moment.)*

She likes Mel Gibson. She sees how much the gun kicks, she's afraid. But she sees I'm not afraid. Then I say, I've got something that doesn't kick so much. And I take out a little 32. And then…I put up the human target. I put the gun in her hand, stand behind her, hold her hands while she shoots. We hit the cord, the human target starts coming at her; she shoots, and it's still coming at her, and she shoots, and it's still coming at her and she shoots, and she shoots, and she shoots. The target doesn't stop till it's right on top of her. She's trembling. And there's bullet holes in the heart. Know what she does? I swear to God; she laughs. She's got a rush like she hasn't had since her professor. When I drop her off, *she* asks *me* for a second date. So we go out again, she mentions, just in passing, she wouldn't mind shooting again. When we use the human target this time? It's gonna happen. I stand close behind her, but she doesn't want me cupping her hands anymore. When that human silhouette starts coming at her, I lightly cup her breasts. We check the shooting pattern, neither one of us says a word about me touching her. She says, "Let's do it again." Here comes the human target again, she's blasting away, and this time I'm caressing her breasts big time, and she keeps shooting and shooting, and shooting, and shooting. We check the target, she's hit the head and the heart, and she's done it on her own. She's so hot she's ready to do it right there in the stall.

You don't believe me…You will.

Half-Court
Brian Silberman

DAVID: a man looking for someone to share his life with (or so he thinks), 30s
SCENE: Here and now

David has decided to attend a "Men's Gathering" in order to gain a sense of "empowerment." Here, he works up his courage and entertains the group with the tale of an early sexual encounter.

O   O   O

(David, at a Men's Gathering. He is seated on a folding chair, part of a large circle. He stands, addressing the audience, now the members of the men's group.)

DAVID: My name's David...uh...Dave. This is my first time here at a gathering like this, but I feel really...whatever...empowered by you all...I just wanted to say that out front. So...now I'm supposed to say something, right? Something...about myself to give my own sense of...whateverthe...to give you a sense...umm...I'm sixteen and a sophomore in high school. It's October... Halloween...and my brother...he has this girl he's seeing. Her parents are out...so, Doug decides that he wants to go over and hang around with her for a while. For sex. And she wants him to come, except her cousin is staying over and might feel uncomfortable with Dougie there. Like she was out of place. So, my brother gets the idea that I should go with him to keep the cousin entertained while he and Margaret...Margaret was her name...while he has sex with her upstairs. He even says that I could get lucky too, if I play my cards right, seeing how Margaret's cousin is seventeen and from out of town and everything. He gives me this condom and says I should show it to her when I think I'm getting close to having a chance. It'll be a Halloween party, he says. So, we need to dress up. And the only costume I have is this Batman thing from two Halloweens ago. You know, those cheap plastic ones you can buy in the grocery store. But I put it on. And Dougie, he has this gorilla head he's wearing...fucking gorilla head. So, we go to the house and she and her cousin are both dressed up as dolls, those Raggedy Ann ones...We all sit around for a while, watching a movie and talking. And pretty soon Doug and his girl go upstairs. And I could hear him a little, laying it on pretty good. Then after a while it gets quiet.

(There is a slight pause.)

We're all right, the cousin and me. We're watching the movie some more. Cheryl. That's her name. Cheryl, from someplace on Long Island. She's all right too. I mean, no big deal or anything, lookswise. But she has, I remember, for someone her age…real nice, uh…

(He motions to his chest, indicating large breasts.)

I mean, these are movie star breasts Cheryl has. So, we're watching the movie…and she leans over and asks me if I knew what they were doing upstairs. And I say, "Shit yeah I know." Then…then she moves over and starts kissing my ear and pulling on the back of my Batman costume. I mean, she fucking…practically ripped it off me. And I'm sitting there in my socks and underwear with this fucking Batman cape around my neck before I know what's happening. And I'm looking for the rubber Dougie gave me, but it's somewhere on the floor with my costume. And she keeps saying, "Come on, come on" over and over and she's climbing all over me. She takes my hand…and puts it inside her Raggedy Ann shirt and…I mean… that's just it. I'm fucking sixteen and I feel Cheryl's movie star tits and cum all over her Raggedy Ann skirt…and Margaret's parents' couch…and everything in fucking range. It was fucking great. I'm running around the goddamn house naked with the Batman cape around my neck. I keep calling to Dougie upstairs. Calling "Hey Dougie, Hey Dougie" until he comes running down. And I can tell he's pissed at me for ruining his time, but I didn't care. Then Margaret comes down too. She sees the couch and starts screaming at me and running around trying to clean it. And Cheryl, she keeps making all of these derogatory remarks about my sexual experience. And she's trying to wash off her skirt with a sponge. And Dougie…then Dougie starts laughing at me. Throwing his head back and just laughing at me.

(He stops. His voice lowers.)

And all of a sudden I don't feel so good anymore. It gets kind of quiet and they all just stare and I start feeling kind of bad. Like I was going to throw up. It was kind of funny. But, I didn't laugh then, because I didn't feel all that funny at the time. I mean, I ought to have felt like laughing, but I just couldn't.

Half-Court
Brian Silberman

MIKE: a man offering advice to a friend, 30s
SCENE: Here and now

Here, down-to-earth Mike tells his friend, David, the trick of acting as though one is well-endowed when one isn't.

O   O   O

MIKE: Lemme tell you something Dave. You're not my type of guy, you understand? Because I think you're basically an uptight asshole…and…no offense…that you're a pussy. I think you know that about yourself…how you come off and everything. But I'm gonna tell you something…I'm gonna tell you where your problem is. Women. Just a minute. Shut your mouth because I'm gonna help you out…I'm gonna tell you something to help you…And I'm going to tell you because whatever the fuck I think about you, you're a *guy*…and as another guy I owe you that…fair enough?
(He leans back.)
Now I got a small penis. I'll admit it. I'm Irish though and we all got small penises. It's all the drinking we do, shrivels it up. But I'll tell you something…chicks dig us. They do. Now, you hear all this hype about big penises…how chicks like 'em. But that's all it is, *hype*. They'll tell you that size is important to them, that they need that to feel *secure*…for a sense of fuckin' security. But think about it. Put yourself where they are…they've got this big rod coming at them and they're just…just…*overwhelmed* by it all. Now, you don't want that…nobody wants that. That's security? Really they're intimidated. Now, they won't say so, but that's what happens. You got a regular size penis, fine. No problem. They feel normal, you're normal, everything's fuckin' normal. With a little dick though, it's different. Some kind of transformation happens…some kind of…fuckin'…*transformation* happens. Understand? See, they're not intimidated by a guy with a little dick. And really, it makes them think they've got more power in the situation. Makes them feel in control…and they like that…they do…They'll even go out of their way to find one…to find a little dick. You understand…I'm

using reverse psychology. So, when I'm sticking it to a woman…I'm sticking it to a woman. See? Now, I've never seen your penis, Dave. And to tell you the God's truth I'm not really interested in ever seeing it. But just from the way you carry yourself…from the way you carry yourself…I'm pegging you as having a smaller than average joint yourself. This may or may not be true. But it's really not important here. Do you understand what I'm trying to tell you? It's not the issue here. It's not your size, it's your attitude. Okay? And you're walking around with the attitude of a guy with a small penis. You catch my drift? See, I act like a guy with a big penis. You get me?

Him
Christopher Walken

TRUCKER: a king of the road, any age
SCENE: A hash house

Here, a hard-living trucker tells a strange tale of giving a man who may or may not have been Elvis Presley a ride to Graceland a few years after his death.

○   ○   ○

TRUCKER: This was back in '80. I recall because of not only what occurred, but because it was two days before my Momma's birthday and I had to get home. I was on a long haul from the West and fried on uppers, wondering if I'd make it on time. Let me explain. I never touch hitchhikers. The last time I did that, the guy produced an ice pick and menaced me.

[HIM: I come to him at this sad hour.]

TRUCKER: I take drugs to thrive, nothing dark or depressing. I take nothing to kill time or pain, so what I'm about to tell you is not clouded by toxic thoughts. That night I'd stopped for gas. I got out. I thought I saw a man in the woods. He was carrying a bundle and he had on a hat, the kind pimps wear. I don't know why, I noticed this man, the quality of him. I paid, and he was gone. And I neared the highway, there he was again in my lights, his back to me, not even thumbing. I put on the brakes "Hop in", just like that. To this day, I don't know what got into me. He got in, we drove about an hour not a word between us. I forgot to mention it was cold out. It was Christmas time as well as my momma's birthday. "Going home for the holidays?" "Yes sir, I'm goin to see my Momma and Daddy". I noticed he had a deep voice. I couldn't see his face on account of that floppy hat. We talked. He was a polite man. Everything finishing up "Yes sir" this and "No sir" that. I thought this must be a man with a good upbringing.

[HIM: I thank Mama and Daddy for that. There's a lot wrong with that couple, but there's a lot right too.]

TRUCKER: Well, I was tired for the rest of the run, but with the coffee and the pills and all in me, I kept awake, my rider and I batting the breeze. I don't recall what we talked about, there was talk about music 'n he said he was looking forward to seeing his mother and father. I could tell he felt about his mother the way I feel about mine. I could tell they were real close. He told me he had presents for his parents in the package he was carryin' and he told me he'd been a truck driver, he did know a lot about cars. Said he had several Cadillacs. I didn't believe that. Thought he was just a poor boy trying to look big. We got along though. I immediately felt there was a comfortable type of thang between us. I told him I'd been having trouble with alcohol. He seemed very understanding and told me he'd had trouble with pills and painkillers. So he knew how I felt. And I sensed immediately that he was a friend. All the time, it had been dark in the cab 'n I hadn't had a look at his face. A few miles outside of Memphis, it started to brighten up, from the lights along the road and I could see him. I could tell he looked familiar. I, uh, I had never gotten around to introducing myself, and uh, I wanted to know who he was, so I said: "My name is Mel." And I glanced over, just as I looked at him, he turned toward me, looked straight into my eyes and said "I'm Him." I was shakin. He said he wanted to be let off. I had to stop the truck anyway, I was so scared. I'd never been to Graceland but two weeks later I went back 'n it was real close, it turns out, to the place where I left him off.

Well, I had six bucks in my pocket so I went to Graceland, it was awful. Must be like going to the Pyramids, every rip off artist in creation trying to charge you separately for something else. Them fuzzy crosses that look like they are made out of blue toilet bowl brushes all over the spot where him and his mom and daddy are buried, 'n the tombstone with his middle name spelled wrong, 'n the flea market across the street. It was vulgar.

[HIM: I own that property. Every stall, every T-shirt, every glass capsule of concert sweat. Everything. The whole thang, it's all mine. In perpetuity.]

TRUCKER: The scene did not move me. Except one thing that did. I was standing there, staring at the blue brush crucifixes, in disbelief when I hear a distinctive voice say "thank you very much". I turned, there's a cage with a magnificent red parrot in it. The keeper said it was His favorite pet. He kept a lot of exotic creatures around the place. These birds live a long time and His favorite looked lonesome tonight. The creature gave me a powerful lost and abandoned look. A fate that bird did not deserve. She missed him deeply in her bird's eye. I bet He never kept her in a cage. There was a guy who claimed to be Himself's cousin. Who, for a dollar, would show you three of His pubic hairs. They were in a little Chinese red lacquer bowl with a gold lid. Maybe they were real. Maybe they were his.

Kept Men
Richard Lay

DAVE: an unemployed advertising executive, 30s
SCENE: New York City, present

Here, Dave tells the story of the day he and his wife first met.

O   O   O

DAVE: Love at first sight. We got stuck in an elevator. The lights went out…just the two of us. Well, can you imagine…we tried all the emergency buttons. Nothing happened. We were on the 35th floor. For 45 minutes we made small talk and prayed that the elevator wouldn't plummet and kill us. Then suddenly she was silent. I said "Are you OK Marcia" because we had exchanged names after 10 minutes. There was a pause and she said "No, I have to pee."…It could have been worse and I said something like…"Go ahead I won't look," It was pitch dark anyway. She was embarrassed about doing it on the floor and it was winter and I was wearing a…hat. So I did what any gentleman would do—let's just say she borrowed my hat.

[CINDY: *(Lights a cigarette.)* A match made in heaven.]

DAVE: Anyway, she sent back the dry-cleaned hat with a bunch of sweet-smelling roses and a note. In the dark I had given her my address and her lawyer's mind had remembered it. The note said "We must do that again sometime." Five months later we were married. She's not a bad woman, she just has this attitude. She can't have kids, so she takes it out on me. I don't mind, I love her. She hurts inside and I hurt for her. So as you can see…we have a perfect marriage.

Kept Men
Richard Lay

PHIL: an unemployed mob hitman, 30-40
SCENE: New York City, present

Here, Phil describes the pleasure he finds in the act of killing someone he doesn't know.

O   O   O

PHIL: There is nothing as beautiful as killing somebody you don't know. You know they done something wrong and deserve to be put down but they never tell the hit man what his victim did to offend. It's important to me that the person doesn't look me in the eye. He might plead for his life…and if I ever thought twice about it he might kill me. Don't get me wrong. When I'm not working I'm a nice person. I give to panhandlers and help blind people cross the road. After a whack I like to go to Joey's Diner and have a plate of eggs and hash smothered with ketchup. I always leave the gun at the scene. It shows disrespect for the guys in homicide…cos when they check out the gun it's one of their own. They don't investigate too hard after that. Paulie says I have a sense of humor. I wouldn't say that but anyone who is the best at what they do has a little pride and an ego that needs to be fed by a little self-induced jocularity.

Metamorphoses
Michael Winn

RANDYE MOOGLAIR: a twenty-something African-American male who doubles as a Diana Ross impersonator

SCENE: Washington, DC

Randye is a world-weary drag queen whose indomitable spirit keeps him going from day to day. Here, we join Randye as he prepares for a performance and celebrates his love of Diana Ross.

○   ○   ○

RANDYE: As you probably have guessed by now,
I am a drag queen.
Some people will say female impersonator,
illusionist,
working girl,
performer,
and so on and so on,
but a rose by any other name,
is a lily.
But, I am a drag queen,
in the colorful tradition of the word.
I am a queen and it's a drag.
Having to put all this shit on.
Thank god I am not a woman
and have to go through this everyday.
Being a drag queen is hard work,
first getting dressed
and having to tuck it.
Try doing a Janet Jackson number with your,
you know what,
taped between your legs
and you will appreciate RuPaul and the rest of us.
I didn't set out to become a drag queen, though.
It was not my ambition,

but my wallet that urged it on.
Well, I am an aspiring writer.
In code that means unemployed writer,
employed waiter.
Well, writing has been a mild success for me
and I was on the reader's circuit
when I went to Follies
and saw this man do Diana Ross
and got hundreds of dollars in tips alone
and I was hooked.
Thank you Diana Ross.
She is the Patron saint of Black Drag Queens across America.
Fuck Judy,
Liza
and Marilyn Monroe.
It is the boss!
Not ole fake assed Bruce Springstein either
but Diana
call her Miss Ross.
She was the one that gave glamour pigment.
I love her!
With all those wigs
and pink lipstick
she let us know that the stage has no definite color.
First with the Supremes
touring across the country with everybody,
black or white,
yelling Diana,
Diana,
Dianaaaaaaaa.
Oh, Miss Ross,
Miss Ross,
Miss Ross,
I love you Miss Ross.
My queendom for Miss Ross.
I remember her at her concert in Central Park.
She was just singing

and singing
and it started raining
and raining
and she kept singing.
A lesser girl would have covered up that weave and gone home.
But not the Boss.
She kept singing
and singing
and singing
and singing
and that rain just matted that weave to her head.
And it was like…
like…
seeing god.
And she kept singing.
Until it started lightning and thundering.
Then she got her ass off stage.
But she came back,
and we came back
to see her again.
Ooh,
I just love her.
Remember Mahogany,
with her and old fine assed Billy Dee
and she was dripping candle wax all over herself.
Child, I burned all the candles in the South.
Thank God there wasn't a black out
or we woulda all been up shit creek.
Even in a wheelchair
or playing a schizophrenic,
or playing Billy Holiday on drugs,
Diana is the boss.
We love you
Miss Millionaire Diana,
and we don't even care if that is Barry Gordy's child,
we still love you
and we know why.

Because you are
D
I
A
N
A.
And that my dears means *everything*.
Work it Miss Ross.
(Lights down.)

Middle-Aged White Guys
Jane Martin

MOON: 46, a mercenary
SCENE: Present, a dump

Mona, Roy's abused wife, is firing at Ray when Moon appears and tells her to "cool it."

○　　　○　　　○

MOON: Shut up, Roy. Now ma'am, I'm a brute killer for pay, and they tell me I'm one of the dozen best shots in the world, left-handed or right. May I call you Mona? Mona, what you're holdin' there is a Rossi 518 Tiger Cat Special, accurate up to about 40 feet and combined with your understandable emotion and inexperience, you most likely won't hit me, whereas, my first couple of rounds will tear off your wrist, leavin' you with one hand for the rest of your life. They tell me the pain's unendurable unless we cauterized it with fire, and by the time we got some kindlin', you'd likely bleed to death. It's strange when you can see right inside your own body like you can when an extremity's gone. We never know what we are because we're covered with skin. Once you find out, you realize we're just walkin' meat. Now I'd feel more comfortable if you'd point that thing at Roy, if you don't mind.
(She does.)

The Midnight Hour
James Campbell

JAMES BALDWIN: African-American novelist, essayist and dramatist, 54
SCENE: St. Paul de Vence, France, April 4, 1978

On the tenth anniversary of the death of Martin Luther King, Baldwin, now an expatriate living in France, describes a dream that he had about King.

O   O   O

JAMES BALDWIN: *(Onstage.)* I was having a conversation about Martin. I can't remember everything that was being said, exactly, but I could see the other people in the room very clearly. I could feel the weight of what they said, if you see what I mean—isn't that strange? Bad things, about Martin; nasty things, ugly things. There were two FBI men—spooks—in hats—and my secretary from the early sixties, Max, was there. And you too, you were there too, Alan. And you thought the FBI must be looking for me. And then all of a sudden, the FBI agents began to sink into the floor—y'know—and sort of…turned into Martin. It was like he sprouted out of their shit-filled guts, something beautiful. And all of a sudden we were, like, having a conversation, him and me, y'know, just like we always used to. Isn't that weird? He said, Jimmy, I'm dead and gone—no, I think he said: I'm dead but I'm not *gone*—but, he said, you're still here, you're on the case. And it was like he was handing me the baton, y'know, to carry on with. *Get on the road.* And he said, Jimmy, don't even read what the critics say…And this is funny because if you knew Martin, he would never use a word like this, but in the dream he said it: he said, these *muthafuckas* can't even read themselves. That's what he said. He said: You've got to teach them how to read. And that's it. That's what I'm here for. That's what any artist is here for. *(Pours a drink and lights a cigarette. For a moment seems to be thinking very intensely of something else. He addresses the telephone.)* Alan, come home…Call me. Or something. *(Pause.)* Lord, I have to get to work. Like Martin said in the dream…*(Chuckles.)* In his dreammmmm…It was amazing, it was like he just rose out of the earth and stood, a colossus, one foot on top of each of those two little men in hats, pushing them down under, burying them. Then suddenly he was *(With a clap of the hands.)* gone. It's been ten years. And before him—Malcolm. And before him—Medgar. And now there's only me. I'm the only one left. Medgar…Malcolm…Martin…*(Pause.)* And me. *(Looks toward the ceiling.)* So come and get me Mr. FBI man!

My Virginia
Darci Picoult

Dan: a man whose wife is terminally ill, 30-40
Scene: Here and now

Julie's illness has been long and devastating but Dan has stood by her every step of the way. When someone finally asks him how he is feeling, he describes the horror of having to watch the one you love die a slow and agonizing death.

O   O   O

Dan: How am I doin? Jeez no one ever asks how I am doin.
Jist "How's Julie…How's Julie…How's Julie…"
How am I doin?! Fine. Fine.
What do you expect me to say?
I was supposed to grow old with this lady. Not have her grow old
in front of my eyes at 34 years of age.
I could deal with her losin her reproductive organs.
I could even deal with her losin her vagina.

Course I couldn't talk about it with any of my buddies.
It was too embarrassin. But at least I had her to talk to.
And in a strange way I felt lucky. Cause some of my buddies
aren't that close to their wives.
So, when the doctor said "This was it"…that there was nothing left
she could do…I punched a hole in the wall. I did.
The whole family sent me to therapy…said I wasn't dealin with
my anger. But at least I am dealin! At least I am not pretendin
that this is part of God's ways. That this is to be expected.
That is loony. And I'll tell you another thing that's loony:
I made my money off of cancer. That's right.
One out of four bodies that came into my home, pardon me,
I mean, my funeral home, died of cancer.
It made me a rich man. But now it is wipin me out.
Cause…I…don't quite know what I am goin to do without her.

She is some lady.
Jist the other night the pastor was here and right in front of him
Julie asked me to pick out her coffin.
I stood there like Atlas but my knees were givin way.
I said "I am goin to pick you out the very best cause I still have
the connections".

New England

Richard Nelson

Tom: a British acting coach living in New York City, 40
Scene: A farmhouse in western Connecticut

While visiting his ex-sister-in-law's country home, Tom is caught up in a domestic tragedy. Here, he does his best to entertain a room full of grieving fellow Brits with a tale of one of his American acting students.

O   O   O

Tom: Another story! A young woman—she's been a model, now she wants to act. So I've asked her to prepare something. Not that I'm going to reject anyone. God forbid that we have standards.

(Paul sets the phone on the table.)

Tom: So she recites: *(American.)* 'Thus do I ever make my fool my purse.' I ask her if she knows what she's saying. She says that *for her* it means—how she shouldn't spend so much money on clothes. She says, *(American.)* 'That may not be what it means to others, but that's what it means to me.'

(Beat.) I ask her: does she know what character she is acting? She says: *(American.)* 'Iago.' Very good. I ask her: did she know that Iago was a—man? She says: *(American.)* 'So what? My last drama teacher—.' 'Drama. Drama.' My favourite American word. 'My last drama teacher said there were no male or female parts anymore—only people parts.' I want to say, I think your teacher could have chosen a better word than 'parts', but I bite my tongue. *(Opens his mouth.)* See? Seven years in this country and there's permanent teeth marks there. *(Continues.)* 'Only people parts.' Interesting. Why not? I say to myself, she's paid in advance. Then about a half hour later, for the hell of it or maybe I'm just wanting to get into the swing of this 'people-part' notion, I say, 'Now that you've done your Iago, what about trying Othello?' *(Beat.)* You'd have thought I'd hit her in the face. *(American.)* 'Othello,' she says in her lovely American, 'I couldn't do Othello.' 'Why is that, my dear?' 'Othello is a black man.' Or is it 'African-American' now? I don't know and I don't give a fuck. Anyway, 'A black man. And only a black man can play a black man.' *(Beat.)* I asked if she felt that was in any way contradictory to what she'd said about 'people-parts'? And she said, she didn't see why it was. *(Pause.)* They don't see themselves. They don't question themselves.

The Only Thing Worse You Could Have Told Me

Dan Butler

MAN: 20-40
SCENE: Here and now

Here, an imaginative romantic takes a moment to offer rhapsodic observations about his sleeping lover.

O   O   O

(We discover a man, lying on the floor, "spooning" with an unseen lover in his bed. It's the deep of the night. The man rolls over to gaze at his sleeping lover. He is beyond bliss. Speaking to the audience.)

MAN: Look at him.

Isn't he beautiful? Can you see?

He is so beautiful.

I just couldn't hold this feeling, I had to share it with someone.

It came out of nowhere. It's true what they say, when you get out of your way and you stop looking for love, then all of a sudden—it's here and it's wonderful and new and easy and…!

Look at him.

He loves me. He loves me.

Someone has that light behind their eyes for me.

And I'm ready for it this time. I'm not shutting it out, my arms are wide-opened. Thank you, God! Thank you, thank you, thank you for inventing love. And touch! And sex!

(The lover stirs.)

Oh, I've gotta be quiet. I don't want to wake him up.

(Looks at him.)

Look at him.

He must be having sweet dreams.

Can you hear him exhale? You hear that? He's broken his nose *three* times. Not from fighting. From falls, during practice. He's a gymnast.

(Pulls back imaginary blanket to show audience his lover's body. Smiles. Then suddenly serious.)

I wonder if he ever looks at me this way.

(All smiles again. Replacing blanket.)

The first time we saw one another, there was that 'click' and we knew.

And we're friends! That's the most important part. Friendship. That's the foundation. Romance comes and goes, but friendship gets you through the...

(Suddenly serious again.)

...everyday.

(Smiles again.)

And you start noticing the little things. Like tonight, he likes to read before he falls asleep. *Lord of the Rings*. He says he's read it hundreds of times since he was a kid, but he never gets tired of it. He just opens the book anywhere and starts reading. I don't know whether you can tell from where you're sitting, but he put his shirt over the lamp so the light wouldn't bother me! It's so sweet!! And it's those little things that add up.

(Gazing back at lover.)

And I watched him read. His eyes got heavy. The book slid out of his hands. I covered him up.

(He does so.)

And there he is 'sleeping beauty'.

And he loves me.

(Suddenly serious.)

And I'm just scared it'll all go away and if I don't know where it came from in the first place then how will I know how to get it back when it leaves?! And then I get mad at him because...

Look at him...he's so relaxed.

He has no idea that this is the only time I can get these things out in the open, when he's asleep.

I know if I showed him this side of me he'd be outa here.

Well I get scared. I get crazy, I get weak. That's a part of me. Of every human being. A part of *him* whether he wants to admit it or not.

We're human!

We're great big wads of contradictions. That's what makes us interesting. If we were all perfect, it'd be boring! But he wouldn't know that because...

Look at him! He's so beautiful!
And how do you *get* beautiful unless you're only thinking of *yourself!?!!*

Oh, God. God, God, God. I didn't realize until this minute how incredibly selfish…*He is!*
He's only thinking of himself. "Only the good times, that's all I want."
Well love, *true* love, is the whole thing. It's good times *and* bad times.

It's trust and patience and time together and weathering storms together and knowing that when bad time do come—and they do; that's life, that's change—that they pass! They pass! And together, *together,* you can make it through anything!!
And this too shall pass.

But right now…I have to take care of myself.
(Lying back down beside his lover.)
I need to take my own time.
And breathe.
And *think*…clearly and dispassionately, whether I really want to consider…
(Looks sadly at lover, then back to audience.)
…a second date.
(He lies back in deep thought as the lights fade.)

Phaedra
Elizabeth Egloff

HIPPOLYTUS: a young man who has just discovered that his step-mother lusts after him, 20s

When Hippolytus is informed of Phaedra's secret passion for him, he reacts with youthful indignation. Here, he attempts to cast her out with a vengeance bordering on violence.

○   ○   ○

HIPPOLYTUS: Well it's finally happened
I have seen the impossible
I have stepped in shit
and heard it sing.

Somebody told somebody
told somebody
we're having an affair
Is that true

Is that a picture of me in your little paw
Do you have a lock of my hair in your bosom
a fingernail in your drawer
Is your love for me the crown of your existence?

Oh Mom
aren't we sick enough
from all this war
but now we have to suffer you.

Ladies and gentlemen
what we have here is a failure of evolution
to properly circumscribe
generation

If what we need is to populate
why not be tulips springing from the soil
trees dropping their fruit
fish politely depositing their eggs

Let's be honest
this whole system is out of whack
Others tie their children up in sacks
and throw them off the pier

but oh not us
We dress them up and educate them
and when they're smart enough
we rape them.

Oh to be what I once was
innocent
innocent
Does anyone remember me

who I was
and where I went?
Never mind. I don't exist.
From now on I'll be nothing more

than a bit of tree
a patch of ground
an idea
an idea

Go, idea.
This is no longer your home.
Find some other hole
to hide your head.

Theseus is gone but not for long
There'll be a day when he'll return
Wait and watch
the way these women will look him in the eye

with what nobility
remove his boots
what honesty
Two timid doves of chastity

Oh I know what you're thinking:
Here's Hippolytus
going on again.
But I had teachers

My teachers said once long ago
these creatures could be trained
could learn to serve Community and God.
Well, now I know:

the monster is just a bitch in heat
and you must learn to master her
your own way
This way for example

your rope around her neck
or better, this:
your boot upon her
throat.

The Professional

Dusan Kovacevic

Translated and Adapted by Bob Djurdjevic

LUKE LABAN: a retired policeman, 50-60
SCENE: A rundown publishing house in Eastern Europe

Luke's professional life was spent conducting the surveillance of Teya Kry, a dissident intellectual considered a dangerous enemy of the state. In the years that he followed Teya, Luke became obsessed with his quarry and saved all of his speeches and stories. Luke's son, a college professor eager to seek intellectual freedom in the West, helped his father to bind all of Teya's writings into several volumes before his own escape. Now that communism has fallen, Luke finds himself out of a job and driving a taxi. Luke seeks out Teya, who is now the head of a publishing house, and presents him with the volumes of his forgotten stories. Here, Luke reveals that in the beginning, he was tempted to kill Teya on several occasions.

LUKE: You asked why I don't talk like a common policeman? Do you have any idea, Teya, how hard I had to work to come to terms with even the most basic concepts of your literary world? Maybe you won't believe me, but I was convinced that Aristotle, Plato, Hegel, Nietzsche, Kafka…and the rest of them—were all foreign secret service agents, that you were seeing and working for…

[TEYA: Which is not far from the truth. I do see them and work for them.]

LUKE: I know that, now. But, imagine someone who has only completed the police academy, like your own father, who then comes up against all these foreign names. To make things worse, in our police records of foreign embassy employees, I found similar names…There was a Huxley, a Tolkien, and a Grass. And when, many years ago, you quoted Sir John Percy, I was convinced that you meant the French cultural attaché. Everything fit, except the cultural attaché didn't write poetry. So I added: "and a poet…" What do you expect? The only foreign names I knew were Engels, Marx, and Lenin.

[TEYA: That story about killing me, was that a joke? You couldn't have been serious…]

LUKE: Deadly serious. God alone saved you. The first time I heard you in the Writer's Club, insulting President Tito at the top of your lungs, I walked out of the club and sat in my car determined to run you over. I waited until morning, but I fell asleep at the wheel…I decided to kill you on several occasions, but as you can see, I have not. Instead, I saved your life, several times, as you can also see. Had I done the former, you'd be gone; had I not done the latter, you'd be gone.

The Professional

Dusan Kovacevic

Translated and Adapted by Bob Djurdjevic

LUKE LABAN: a retired policeman, 50-60
SCENE: A rundown publishing house in Eastern Europe

Here, Luke recalls one of Teya's sardonic tales which has an uncomfortable parallel meaning to his own existence.

O   O   O

LUKE: Yes. One night, at the old bar in the Atelier theatre, you traded your leather jacket for Captain Markovich's binoculars.

[TEYA: Excuse me, but why did I trade my jacket for a pair of binoculars?]

LUKE: Zoran told you to trade them because he said as soon as war breaks out you could instantly become a Major with a pair of binoculars like that. He said that people without binoculars are the first to get killed during a war…That was the night when your story about how to kill grandpa humanely was born.

[TEYA: How to kill grandpa humanely?]

LUKE: Yes…You talked about how various nations deal with the "problem" of their unproductive elderly—people who only eat but don't work. In Yugoslavia the members of a family bake a round, flat, loaf of bread, put it on grandpa's head, and hit the loaf with a big rock. The Eskimos, on the other hand, take their old folk fishing out on the ice, cut a hole in the ice, give them a fishing rod and return next year to see what they have caught. In the mountainous regions of Japan, when the first snow comes, the eldest grandson puts grandpa on his back and carries him to the top of a mountain. He leaves him there in a sitting position to wait for spring…then, Radmilovic said that, where he comes from, they do away with the old men most humanely. He said "They take grandpa by the hand, take him to a freeway, and let a chicken loose on the road." Then they say: "Catch the chicken, Grandpa!"

The Psychic Life of Savages
Amy Freed

DR. ROBERT STONER: American Poet Laureate, 60s
SCENE: Here and now

After a long drunken weekend, the cantankerous Dr. Stoner turns on his young protégé and debunks his intellectual pretensions in a passionate outburst.

O   O   O

STONER: Understand the language of the birds? I've woken up to hear them plotting on my life! Miracles! You fool! You don't know the utter horror of miracles! I take 3,000 milligrams of lithium a day to keep me from walking on water, and sometimes I do it anyway!

[TED: I'm sorry—I didn't mean…]

STONER: You think all creation's some big Hindu illusion? You wing-growing bastard. Turn yourself into a goddamn bald eagle. And I hope some teenager pops you with his daddy's shotgun.

[ANNE: Testy! Testy!]

STONER: Think you're the first man to dream of wings? You've never experienced the horrible freedom of the winged mad. You want a miracle? Try this one! One and one make two! But you won't stop till they make three! Or cat!

[TED: Bob—Father, you're excited. I think you misunderstand what the Zen-masters are saying.]

STONER: I'm saying have the guts to call a spade a spade, recognize the cold hard law of gravity for what it is, which is the grace of God—recognize how many angels are at work each day insuring that Newton's apple continues to fall down, down, down, not up into the ozone with all your Zuni medicine men flapping around as bats and hoot-owls along with *me* when I forget to take my pills! Have the guts to give glory to the truth!

(Quietly.)

If only that, we should have the guts to give glory to what truths we can.

The Psychic Life of Savages
Amy Freed

TED MAGUS: a young English poet, 30s
SCENE: Here and now

Here, the pretentious poet/professor regales his students with his own special insight into the process of creating poetry.

O   O   O

TED: Yes. The ending was a nightmare. I wrestled with it for weeks, like Jacob wrestling the Angel. Finally, I dreamed it. I saw the slug dying, covered with salt by a vicious housewife. As clear as day, I dreamed him, a big quivering mass of slop and mucus writhing in the rotted mulch…and I found the final lines…"And bubbling there, I'm left alone, a bitter pool of fragrance, shrinking in the sun."

[ALL THE GIRLS: Wow. Oh, that's incredible. I cried when I—]

TED: So. What have we learned? Don't be polite. Don't be small. Poetry is not all rose gardens and my cat with last year's dead leaves, you know. We're talking about the dark side. The unmentionable terrors. The unspeakable joys. What are yours? Show me. I know my fears are…shedding tears in public, showing affection for other men…in a physical way, you know, hugging, wrestling, that sort of thing, and—Hah! Dancing!—I mean why—dancing? It terrifies me. My own twisted ideas of manhood, I suppose, as passed down from one generation of small, cramped men to another, when—my God! The blood of our ancestors *thrummed* with the dance. A good jig, a leap under the moonlight—the hunt, the rites of mating or of death—oh come! Let's…tango! Who wants to jump in first?

Rain
Garry Williams

Staff: 40s, ex-farmer
Scene: Present, dusk, farmhouse porch

Staff tells about his recent fall from the roof which left him confined to a wheelchair.

$\bigcirc$ $\bigcirc$ $\bigcirc$

STAFF: Is that life? Is it really that simple? 'Cause I thought mine out. All of it. My whole life. On the way off the barn roof. You know they say your life flashes before you? Well, it doesn't flash. It takes as long the second time as it does the first. But it's all there, like some long boring home movie that someone's making you sit through. And you keep saying to yourself, why the hell did I do that? I mean, every decision you ever made is right there and you're saying, why the hell did I do that? And the thing that's scary is that you can't do anything to change it. All you can do is watch. And you start to wonder if it's that way the first time around too. Anyway, I figured as soon as I'd watched the whole thing it'd be over, you know? I'd see myself climb up on the barn, drop the hammer, reach for it like an asshole, start to slide, say to myself, why the hell did I do that, and then I'd hit the ground. But it didn't happen. I went through everything in my life and I was still falling. Hours, it seemed, I figured I'd probably lost track of time, you know, but the longer I fell the more I started thinking—maybe I don't have to hit at all. If I haven't hit yet, maybe it's because of something I'm doing. And this thought went through my mind. It said, "I think, therefore I am." And I couldn't remember where I'd heard that before, but at that point I didn't give a shit where I'd heard it—I thought that was the key. As long as I was thinking, I wasn't going to hit the ground and stop being. So I thought my brains out. I ran through batting averages, tried to list every car I ever owned, named damn near every kid in my sixth grade class. Then I started thinking about you. Hell, just trying to figure you out kept me afloat longer than anything else. I came to two decisions about you on my way off that barn. One, you're probably the best person I've ever known in my life. And two, you're doing it all just because you think you're supposed to. That's why you didn't leave me a long time ago when you should have, because somewhere in the Bible it says you're not supposed to. It's why you would never put Ty in a home. And it's why you took care of my mom for twelve years. That woman never had a kind word to say to you, but you let her live in your house for twelve goddamn years. And you know why? Because that's what God would want you to do. *(Slowly.)* And that…got me thinking about God. That was my big mistake. Because as soon as I got to thinking about God I thought, hey, now might be a pretty good time to pray. I hadn't prayed in twenty or thirty years, you know, but as far as I could remember, it was a lot like thinking. So I thought, okay, I'll just pray for awhile here. But then, just like always happened to me even back when I was little—I couldn't think of anything to pray about. There's that little moment when you wonder what the hell you're doing. Are you talking to yourself? Or are you really talking to some being up there somewhere who created you and knows everything you think and do? And if that's the case, what do you have to say that he doesn't already know? And if you're gonna pray for something, like to not die, are you trying to get him to change his mind? I mean, did he already decide you were going to die, but you ask him not to let you die, so he goes, "Oh…okay." You start wondering this shit, at least I do. And I always did, you know? So just like before, I hit that point where I kind of blank out about what it was I was gonna pray about. You know, your mind just kind of goes blank for a second. And that was all it took. Next thing I know I'm looking at a hospital ceiling.

Safe House
WM. Seebring

BOB: a psychotic lawman, 50s
SCENE: A cop's home

When his wife is visited by distant relations, Bob is delighted to be put in charge of a pot-smoking, teen-aged hell-raiser. Here, he delivers his first warning to the errant youth.

○   ○   ○

BOB: You don't fool me, punk. I know who you are and I know *exactly* what you're up to.

[ANDY: Okay, okay. Ease up, will ya? No one got hurt, alright?]

BOB: Maybe not. But one of these days you'll be on one of your high-flying trips to Venus or Mars, speeding down some county road, like that one past Buck's Do-Me-Inn, out there where that little curly haired girl lives with her Ma and six chickens. That little girl, she'll be out front, all dressed up purty in her shiny, patent leather shoes and her gingham frock under which she'll be wearing a pair of them little pink cotton undershorts, the kind with them squirrelly little rosettes sewed all around the waistband and she'll be playing with this ball she's got, a bright red bouncy ball, *a present she got from Santy Clause.*

(Beat.)

When all of a sudden, that little red ball tumbles out of her tiny little hands and it rolls across that dusty, dirty road. Well the little girl, she wants to get that little ball back see…but first, first she stops and she looks both ways like her Ma taught her and she don't see nothing coming so she takes just one little tiny innocent step when…*Splat!* You'll run her down like she was some Godless mongrel cur-dog! Well I'm the lawman that cleans it up! But not your mess, punk. Not this time.

(Beat.)

You got me, druggie-boy?

Sanctuary

David Williamson

BOB KING: an internationally renowned investigative journalist, late 40s
SCENE: A luxury housing estate in the north of Australia

John has pushed Bob to the limit of his physical and spiritual endurance, causing the tortured man to finally confess the horror that forced him into retirement.

○   ○   ○

BOB: OK, you're not impressed, but a much bigger test was coming up. I was, by now, one of the Army tribe. The Colonel began to take me out on military patrols. I wrote a piece about the experience, but I didn't write everything. I didn't write that they gave me a gun and they even allowed me to fire it. I'm sure I didn't hit anything but all my warrior fantasies were let loose. There I was stalking through the jungle, fighting the bastards who were trying to turn Guatemala into another Cambodia. The truth was it wasn't very dangerous because there weren't many guerrillas out there, but it was terrific fun. The hunting pack male bonding—the sheer exhilaration of it took me by surprise. They drank toasts to me, slapped me on the back and told me I was 'un macho'—a real man. I was fearless, tough and a great, great friend of Guatemala. By now, as you've noted, everything I wrote was pro-Government and my editor back home was very pleased. And I was very pleased with myself that I wasn't some left liberal cowardly excuse for a journalist propping up a hotel bar like the rest of them. I was a latter day Hemingway out there on the front line. Then one night the Colonel and I got very drunk and he put his arm around my shoulder and said, 'Of course you're not seeing the real war.' 'Show it to me,' I said. 'Impossible,' he said. 'It can never be written about.' I swore to him that if he showed me the real war I would never, never write about it. He cut his arm then mine and while the blood flowed I swore on oath. He took me on the 'real' war next morning.
[JOHN: You must've known what he was talking about.]
BOB: Yes, I knew exactly what he was talking about, and the appalling things is that I got a prickly, almost sexual surge of excitement thinking about it. I didn't want to kill. I just wanted to see it done.

[JOHN: You wanted to see people die?]

BOB: *(Suddenly angry.)* It's only a few centuries since public hangings used to draw hundreds of thousands. It's only two millennia since people flocked to the Colosseum. It killed Roman drama stone dead. People preferred to go and watch men kill each other. Do you think because your universities teach phony courses in human perfectibility that we're any different at core!
(Bob calms himself.)

I was curious. How do people cope with imminent death? How would I cope? I wasn't sadistic, just insatiably curious. Just before dawn they rounded up a dozen teachers. Security had photographed them speaking at a rally to insist the Government curb the death squads. Very quick, very simple. Bash on the door, break it down if there was no answer. Drag them off with their families screaming in terror. Throw them handcuffed in the back of a big military truck. Nine men five women. We were all wearing balaclavas.

[JOHN: Was it exciting?]

BOB: No, it was ugly. I looked at the teachers. They knew what was going to happen. They were numb with terror. We stopped at a clearing a long way out of town at dawn. No one seemed in a hurry. The teachers were left in the back of the van. My comrades sounded jocular, cheerful. The Colonel came over to me with a smile on his face and told me that sex was nothing compared with what he was going to offer me now. He handed me his revolver and told me I could have my pick. He said to make sure I made them beg for at least five minutes in order to get the full charge. He said there was nothing like the euphoria of absolute power of life and death.

(John gets to his feet, staring at Bob in horror. He feels nauseous. He grabs the phone, and goes to the bathroom where we hear him being ill. The toilet flushes and he returns.)

BOB: *(Quietly.)* They dragged a woman up to me. She was begging for her life already. I looked in her eyes dropped the gun, ran to the edge of the clearing and was violently ill. My 'buddies' laughed loudly.

[JOHN: Did you watch them kill?]

BOB: No, but I heard it all. The begging, the taunting, the vile abuse and the final shot. The Colonel came over to me and told me there was one left. It had been decided that unless I killed, I myself would be killed because they weren't going to risk this story ever being published. He put the gun back into my hand and led me across. It was another woman. I started shaking with fear, then just dropped the gun on the ground and said, 'Kill me.' The Colonel raised his pistol to my head and pulled the trigger. The chamber was empty. They roared with laughter. Big joke. The next chamber did have a bullet and the woman was killed before their laughter died. That was the test. I couldn't kill for pleasure. I couldn't even kill to save my life. I took the first plane out the next day.

Self-Defense
Michael P. Scasserra

AGING HIPPIE: 40-60
SCENE: Here and now

Here, a charter member of the Age of Aquarius takes a moment to lambaste life in the 80 s and 90s.

O O O

(An aging hippie-type wearing a bandanna around his head is poking through an ashtray looking for cigarette butts.)
Everyone today's goin' around being all fuckin' selfish and shit
worrying about this self-esteem crap
throwin' out all this fuckin' attitude
and you know what?
People should just shut the fuck up.
Some people don't deserve self-esteem.
Most people don't deserve self-esteem.

People suck.
Like all you people
you people with jobs and houses and cars and all that baggage
pretending to be into the environment
into saving the planet
into patching up the ozone.
So what do you do to take care of all this stuff?
You recycle your Diet Pepsi cans and your paper bags,
like as if this isn't a law already.
Then you feel like you done your part to save the Earth…

…which is doomed anyway, as I see it.

See, I already did my part.
I tried.
I have been recycling bottles since the late seventies.
Of course, that was my career.

68

I used to do it for the deposit money
to eat and stuff while I was on the road,
but back then, this was like social responsibility, too,
the way I see it.

See, I was ahead of my time.
Always have been.
Still am.

I hate my fellow Americans.
You all suck.
See, I choose to stand outside your bullshit.
'Cause I'm secure enough on the inside.
I don't need all of your bourgeois luxuries
like a pair of designer jeans,
a cellular phone,
a mailing address.

The eighties sucked, totally.
I sat 'em out.
One long, Republican-induced pain in my ass.
I still say I'd rather have a lava lamp over track lighting.
Vietnam over Bosnia.
I'd still take Bob Dylan…Dylan!
"How does it feel? To be on your own."
Over Madonna.
Madonna?
See…what the fuck is that all about?
What does that bitch stand for?
Blonde capitalist mother-fucker.
She's a fuckin' yuppie in sheep's clothing.
She's a yuppie in no clothing.
Like she was the first bitch in the world to take off her clothes?
Man, we took off our clothes.
And we did it for free.
It's like my brain goes into complete lapse.
People talk about the sixties coming back
and everything we stood for and ideals and freedom

and what do we get instead?
Tie-dye.
I didn't march on Washington
and burn my draft card
and live for four-and-a-half fuckin' years in a commune
so we could have tie-dye.
I did it for the drugs and the sex and the ideals we shared.
Like we fuckin' need tie-dye again?
I didn't get that shit the first time around,
now I go to the mall, I'm hanging out, and I see all these bleach blonde
bitches wearing tie-dye shirts with Gucci shoes?
What the hell is going on here?

Like the krishnas say…
I forgot what they say.
I was a krishna, though.
this was Berkeley…circa…I don't know.
Late sixties, early seventies.
It's one big blur.
But I joined, and at first I didn't see how I fit in
but I ended up learning a lot about myself…
but they made me plow fields, too.
I remember that.
And they made me get up at five in the morning
like as if real human beings get up at five in the morning.
Yeah…yeah…I got it now.

The krishnas said that if you join them
your life would be simplified
and you would get closer to your spiritual self, you know.
I might have, too,
but between plowing those damn fields and gettin' up at five in the morning, I was entirely too wasted to get in touch with my soul.

But that doesn't matter.
I didn't really need their shit
because I always had self-respect
for myself.

Hey, I got a story for you.
Get this.
I once shook Dylan's hand.
Dylan's hand. I shook.
And he almost fell off the fuckin' stage, man
and he, like, grabbed on to me
for support.
So I like gave him balance, you know.
and with his playing thumb
he gouged a piece of skin right off of my knuckle.
And it bled and got infected
and it got all like purple and shit
and oozy…
man…
it was the greatest fuckin' thing.
Dylan infected me.
I would never let fuckin' Madonna infect me, man.
And something tells me that bitch could do it from thirty paces,

if you know what I'm saying.

See, so, the way I see it,
if I hadn't of been there for Dylan,
he might of fallen off the stage
been impaled on a mike stand or some shit
he'd be dead
and then he wouldn't have been around for Bangladesh,
No Nukes,
Farm Aid.

See, so, I did my part.
But we're all doomed anyway.

"How does it feel?"
"To be on your own?"
(He makes an obscene gesture toward the audience.)
Fuck you.
Feels good.

Sophistry
Jonathan Marc Sherman

IGOR: an introspective college student, 20
SCENE: A New England college campus, 1990

When he is accused of putting the moves on his friend's recent ex-girlfriend, Igor does his best to protect his relative innocence to the young woman in question.

O   O   O

IGOR: I wouldn't even know how to start, Robin, I swear. First of all, trying to find somebody safe on this campus, I mean, somebody who's relatively disease free, who hasn't slept with one of my friends, who isn't heavily involved with somebody, who isn't painful to look at or talk to, who actually likes guys—this is a next-to-impossible task. If I do find somebody like this, the odds that she will have any interest in me are not terrific. And, you know, I mean, I don't even know if I would *allow* myself to go after a person I respected, since I know the kind of guy I am. I know the thoughts I think. I know I would not want *me* to date my daughter, if I had a daughter. I know that I cease to become interested in nine out of ten women almost immediately after I've slept with them, and I've only slept with *three* women. I know I prematurely ejaculate on occasion. I know I sometimes prefer blow jobs to actual intercourse, yet I can't come up with a halfway logical reason for a woman to want to give one. I know I find sleazy women pretty attractive, and look at most women as objects. I know that white men have a hell of a historical legacy, what with enslaving blacks and treating women like cattle, so I feel ashamed to be a member of what is supposed to be the privileged class. And I know that sensitive guys sound good in theory, but in practice, most of the women I observe are attracted to men who treat them like shit. I know these things. So, you see, it would be very difficult for me to try to pick you up while retaining even *minor* amounts of dignity and truth and still enjoy myself a little. *(Beat.)* But I was standing over there, across the room, and I saw Willy try to pick you up, and I know he's pretty smashed tonight, and I just wanted to see if you were okay. *(Beat.)* Are you okay?

Sugar Down Billie Hoak

Brian Silberman

STREET: a coke addict dying of cancer, 40s
SCENE: New York City, the present

Street encounters Boogie, a young hustler who has just stolen a brick of coke, in a subway sta-
tion men's room. A hard-core addict, Street wastes no time in tapping the coke and shooting
up. Now high, Street describes his love of storytelling.

O   O   O

STREET: I like tellin' my stories t'a little kids.

[BOOGIE: 'Cause you're a fuckin' child molester.]

STREET: *(Ignoring the interruption, his voice taking on an hypnotic tone and*
rhythm.) I go where they is. Groups of 'em. The park is good…the play-
grounds…I get 'em together…"Sit in a circle," I tell 'em. They fuckin' do it.
I say, "This story starts with a quiet." Then I'm quiet, see? Real serious. Real
fuckin' intimidatin'. I let it go. Two or three minutes a' quiet.

(He laughs gleefully.)

Still I don't say nothing. It's so fuckin' intimidatin'.

(Slight pause.)

But it ain't an empty quiet, it's a rich quiet. It ain't like being asleep, it's being
awake, lettin' the fuckin' doors open. Now I start to say somethin'. Real
calm. Slow. And I let it go, like it unfolds or somethin'. Slow at first, but it
gets bigger and bigger, 'til talking's like flyin' and I'm risin' to these mother-
fuckin' heights, like I ain't never gonna come down. 'Til I can see fuckin'
God.

(There is a slight pause. He begins to cry softly.)

That's why you always got this sad feeling in your gut at the end of a story.
'Cause at that time there's a lotta things going on in the head a the people
you're talkin' to. They're mixin' their ideas with yours, makin' these connections. Everything's movin', like you're engaging a fuckin' clutch in their
heads. But your job's over. You gotta fuckin' go. 'Cause everything from then
on is in their heads. You ain't gotta be there no more. You ain't needed. They
don't want you. It's like you're just the fuckin' needle. You're the needle they

got their fix through and they toss you out like some piece of shit in the toilet.

(He pauses.)

That's when you feel your basic thing, your basic condition, like all the other fuckin' poets and storytellers…loneliness. It's loneliness.

(Street begins shaking slightly, a tremor from the cocaine. He lowers his voice and his gaze. It is touching, what he has just said, and he seems to know it. A small smile forms on his lips.)

If you're lucky though…if you're fuckin' good enough…if your fuckin' muse is smilin' at you, you'll be off on another one, another story. You'll get another fix for them and they have t'a come back. 'Cause you got the power. You may just be the needle, but they depend on ya. They crave ya in their skin. So they come…and for another little time you'll be in real connection with your people and your maker…you will be redeemed.

Talk/Show
Michael P. Scasserra

MAN: watching television
SCENE: Here and now

Channel surfing becomes a metaphor for life in the following exaltation of the power of using the remote control.

$$O \qquad O \qquad O$$

CHANNEL SURFER: *(A man with a remote control.)*
I'm totally into self-programming
making choices
that
in essence
I mean I realize that when I'm clicking
it's like
the instrument of ease
I don't know if it was designed that way
but it seems to dovetail very nicely
with just getting people to just sit around
and be on their own for the next five hours
and that same instrument of ease
which has facilitated
you know
coach-potatoing
at the same time
it creates a kind of
unaware rebellion from programming
I'm a big zapper
I zap like ten
just zillions of times at any given time
but see I refuse to be like the people who
are being herded through television
through these corridors
to

to
to
and it's not a Machiavellian kind of thing
it's more like
you know
a catch-22
part of that whole unconscious thing
where nobody's really taking responsibility
programmers or viewers
everybody's just surfing
on their own
on the flow of the televised text
and what's become very symbolic to me is
people getting very cued-out and fragmented
collectively unconscious
in a weird sort of way
I have the television on all the time
I think I get a lot out of that
but it can be dangerous
because you're sort of staking out this
blind canyon of confusion
again, not in a Machiavellian sense
but by having so much opportunity to
click off
to escape the emotional momentum
that can be a good thing
a very good thing
or bad
if you break away from the whole of
the thing
you might be doing yourself a disservice
but you might, um
see moments out of the whole
which are more clear and enlightening
like if you're watching
"The Amy Fisher Story"
um

I think it might have been
even more interesting to have
the first "Amy Fisher Story' ran on ABC
then a week later CBS and NBC ran theirs
simultaneously
and I think it would have been
a lot of fun
although I did not watch
"The Amy Fisher *Story*"
in a strict sense
I did spend some time switching back from
channel 2 to channel 4
channel 2 to channel 4
and I think it would have been
a
lot
of
fun
if channel 7 had been running theirs
simultaneously
and in that sense
I have no interest in "The Amy Fisher Story"
I don't find it
very interesting to begin with
but instead of mindlessly watching
"The Amy Fisher Story"
and becoming one of the masses
see
I refuse to just eat what's put before me
I want to pick and choose
I want to find the connections
I don't want some faceless person
doing that for me
because of
the whole idea that
truth is relative
and your programming should be your own.

The Ties that Bind

Regina Taylor

MALICE: a tough-talking man with twisted insight into the relationship between men and
women, 30-40

SCENE: A street corner

Here, Malice makes love to a photo in a magazine.

O   O   O

MALICE: *(Reading a magazine.)* Michele, I told you before—don't be wearing that Spandex shit. You're a big star—too big a star to be showing yourself in that shit. I told you—quit that shit. Now listen to me. And call me on Wednesday. *(He flips a page.)* Hey, sweetheart. Yeah, I'm talking to you! What's your name? Ahh, Sabrina. That's a pretty, pretty name. You like movies—uh—huh. Old movies—me too. We should go see a movie sometime—you know, maybe walk in the park. You'd like that. Or take a boat ride. Yeah?—Yeah—Oh, you are just too funny. Stop. You are just too funny. *(He licks the page.)* I'm not moving too fast am I? Come home with me. Meet the parents. *(He rips out the page and stuffs in into his pants.)* Sabrina…*(To Walter.)* This is a private moment, thank you. You some kind of pervert? What you think you lookin' at?

(Walter turns away.)

Never mind him, Sabrina. Make yourself at home. There's a Coke in the fridge…no, over there on the right. *(Back to the magazine.)* I am tired of you. You have the nerve to show your face again—Lie to me again—"no new taxes…" *(Punches magazine.)* Tell me another—"no government intervention…"*(Punches magazine again.)* I told you…*(Takes out nail clippers and stabs magazine.)* Lying to me—Can't lie without a tongue. I can't hear you now, joker. Joker, I can't hear you. Can't lie without a tongue, can you, can you—what—can you? *(He flips page.)* I hated that joker…Yeah, I'm doing fine, and you? Haven't seen you in a while…just hanging, you know…and you…damn, thought you was dead…*(Turns to Walter.)* And what are you reading, man?

The Ties that Bind
Regina Taylor

MALICE: a tough-talking man with twisted insight into the relationship between men and
women, 30-40
SCENE: A street corner

Malice here informs an acquaintance that he should have married a white woman.

O   O   O

MALICE: See, niggers don't know. White folks know the game. A black
woman always wants you to be proving something. It's a cultural thing. Sister say, Oh you think you successful—you may be successful but don't come
this way with that successful crap. Think you running something 'cause I got
news for you—You have to prove to me why I should be giving you my time
and energy. Tell me why you want to be with me and you better be con-
vincing. White women—they come at you a little different. They like to rub
you the right way. Hey, sweetheart—you are successful. I want to be with
you 'cause you are successful. The game is how do I get you and keep you
happy. That's part of their culture. White folks give you credit. They'll suck
your butt, let you know you are the baddest cat around. They show you
appreciation. Invite you yachting. Come on, man, go golfing with us this
weekend. We appreciate you. Who you are. Be with us…Be one of us…Be
us. And as long as you do that do—it's groovy. You know what I'm saying.
You are in and it is groovy. You know.

Tough Choices for the New Century

Jane Anderson

BOB DOOLEY: 30s-40s
SCENE: Southern California, Present

Bob Dooley runs seminars about safety during natural disasters. Here he works the audience over pretty well.

O   O   O

BOB: OK. I'm going to bring out the next speaker, but what I'd like you to do while we set up is for you to take a little mental tour of your house or apartment. In your mind's eye, look at all the things you have on your shelves—picture frames, souvenirs from your vacation, that set of commemorative dishes that you never eat on, trophies, the clay dog your child made in kindergarten, that glass jar filled with pennies, that jumbo bottle of scotch your office chums gave you on your birthday. *Now imagine all these objects being hurled across the room at your head at sixty miles per hour.* Or imagine a wave of fire tearing through your bedroom, spreading over your bed, the blankets the bed spread, all those dopey little frou-frou pillows that you have to throw off to get to the real pillows—imagine all of it starting to smoke in the terrible heat then Whoosh, exploding into flames! And all those crappy plastic knicknacks you keep throwing in a drawer of your bedside table—imagine it all melting into a bubbling, black ooze. And what about that guitar in the closet you never play, that stupid walking stick someone brought you back from Scotland and *baskets,* how many of you keep collecting *baskets*—Whoosh! Or imagine being Noah sailing across the flood-swollen earth. Imagine the miles and miles of muddy, garbage-choked water, people's jetsam floating up, banging up against the side of the ark—KACHUNK, KACHUNK, KACHUNK—spooking all the animals inside, driving you nuts! Or imagine millions and millions of locusts swarming into your living room, devouring everything in their path, slipcovers, curtains, all those coffee-table books you never read—*The Cat Lover's Handbook, (He makes eating sounds.) Hawaii from the Air, (More devouring eating.) The World of Hummel, (He makes extra vicious eating sounds.)* Imagine everything you own or love or *thought* you loved being destroyed in countless other ways. Imagine it all gone. Then ask yourself, "What would I really miss?" *(a beat)* What would I really miss? *(Bob takes his hankie out, wipes his mouth. Quietly.)* OK, terrific.

Water and Wine
Stuart Spencer

BUONARROT of Michaelangelo
SCENE: Winter 1506, a farm outside of Florence

Buonarroti has just come up from the cellar of a farmer, Giovanni, and his son, Enrico, an aspiring artist. Buonarroti responds to Enrico's comment about being an artist like the one who made the sculpture.

O   O   O

BUONARROTI: For God's sake, just shut up, would you?! *(Pause.)* You don't understand, do you. When God made the world, he *created* something. In the truest sense, the real sense of the word: to bring into being. There was nothing, now there is something. That's what God did. We forget that— there was nothing. *Nothing.* And now…the world. The stars, the sun…*(He runs his fingers along the table top and looks at his fingertips.)*…dust, air, stones. You. I. When an artist paints, or a sculptor hammers the stone— that's not creation. We're just rearranging things. It looks new, it seems as if we've created something, but no—never. It's not possible. Only God can create things and he's long since finished. *But…*sometimes, once in a lifetime, once in a thousand years, there is a work of man that *seems* to be new. That seems to be actually created. The material seems not to have been before, and now it is. *(He gestures behind him, to the inner door.)* That…that creation in your cellar is one of these. Laocoon, he's the man, the father, a Trojan priest. He reaches up to escape the serpent's grasp and…*(Unconsciously, he begins to imitate the figures in the statue.)*…his head rears back just at the moment of knowledge, the moment of despair, knowing that the reach is futile. He knows in this instant that he will die in the serpent's terrible grip. And his sons will die too. That all is lost. Yet the moment is about the *struggle*, the agonizing struggle that must go on! Now, and forever. *Now, this precise moment! And forever!* If ever man came close to God, it was in that piece of stone in your cellar. In that marble, man has created something which comes breathlessly close, heartstoppingly close to anything in God's own creation. And you casually stroll out the door and say you'd like to do that too. Well, you can't! It doesn't happen that way! Nobody can! Even *I* can't!

Watbanaland

Doug Wright

PARK: a man driven to despair by the birth of his disabled son, 40
SCENE: Here and now

One night of drunken revelry with his secretary has resulted in the birth of a child with severe birth defects, leaving Park shattered by the realization that the baby's condition was a result of his genetic legacy. In the meantime, his wife, Flo, is desperate for a child of her own. Lashed by guilt, Park cannot bring himself to confess the truth. Instead, he writes everything down in letters that he eats rather than sends. Here, Park struggles his way through one such letter.

O   O   O

PARK: Dear Flo,

They say even the most ardent sadist can still be driven deaf by screams. And so I am writing you this note.

For months, you implored me to give you a child. Surprise, surprise. I already have one. His name is Milo. He lies between us in the bed at night. I reach out to touch you, and he bites my hand. He is as misshapen and voracious as our marriage.

In the nursery, you are surrounded by perfection. Ripped from the labels of Zwieback and Gerber's, gorgeous children, kissed by God. I could not give you less. I feared creating another monster; instead, I became one.

You attempted pregnancy without me. Ha-ha. Hysterical. When there was no resulting baby, you cried into a blue linen handkerchief. I saved that handkerchief. Behind a closed door, Bartok blaring, I cried, too. Our tears mingled in the fabric, the first time we have mixed fluids in years.

I have a final and persistent fantasy. One evening—tonight perhaps—you will walk into the room, ready as always to be hoisted on the rack. Instead I will guide you gently to a chair. On my knees, I will divulge everything. Perhaps—just once—God, grant me this please—our lives will explode in violence. I, tearing at your skirts, heaving sobs; you, bruising me with your fists. Primitive, yes, but not devious. In the end, of course, you will forgive me. Thus purged, I will once again be free. Able to look at you. To touch you in the dark.

You asked once if I loved you. I have that question documented, on tape, in our safe deposit box. The answer? With great pain.